Clinics in Developmental Medicine No. 50

Neonatal Behavioral Assessment Scale

by

T. Berry Brazelton

1973
Spastics International Medical Publications
LONDON: William Heinemann Medical Books Ltd.
PHILADELPHIA: J. B. Lippincott Co.

ISBN 0 433 04030 0

Reprinted 1976

Printed in England at THE LAVENHAM PRESS LTD., Lavenham, Suffolk.

Floppy Infant   Allen Stuckey, MD

NEONATAL BEHAVIORAL ASSESSMENT SCALE

This Manual was developed with the assistance of

Daniel G. Freedman, Ph.D.
Associate Professor, Committee on Human Development
University of Chicago

Frances Degen Horowitz, Ph.D.
Professor Human Development and Psychology
University of Kansas

Barbara Koslowski, M.A.
Research Associate, Center for Cognitive Studies
Harvard University

Henry Ricciuti, Ph.D.
Professor Human Development
Cornell University

John S. Robey, M.D.
Clinical Associate in Pediatrics
Harvard Medical School

Arnold Sameroff, Ph.D.
Associate Professor Psychology, Pediatrics and Psychiatry
University of Rochester School of Medicine

Edward Tronick, Ph.D.
Research Associate Children's Hospital Medical Center
Boston, Massachusetts

T. Berry Brazelton, M.D. is Clinical Assistant Professor in Pediatrics
at Harvard Medical School

The photographs were taken by Denise Zioahlen and Edward Tronick

Contents

PREFACE   *Martin Bax and Ronald Mac Keith*   ix

FOREWORD   1

INTRODUCTION
State assessment. Order of presentation and general procedure. Scoring. Examiner training.   4

THE MANUAL
State observations   13
Response decrement to light   13
Response decrement to rattle   16
Response decrement to bell   16
Response decrement to pinprick   17
Orientation response—inanimate visual   19
Orientation response—inanimate auditory   21
Orientation—animate visual   21
Orientation—animate auditory   23
Orientation—animate visual and auditory   24
Alertness   24
General tone—predominant tone   26
Motor maturity   26
Pull-to-sit   27
Cuddliness   29
Defensive movements   30
Consolability with intervention   33
Peak of excitement   34
Rapidity of buildup   34
Irritability   35
Activity   36
Tremulousness   36
Amount of startle during exam   37
Lability of skin color   38
Lability of states   40
Self quieting activity   40
Hand to mouth facility   41
Smiles   43
Elicited responses   43
Passive movements of arms and legs   44
Descriptive paragraph   44

EXAMPLES OF DESCRIPTIVE PARAGRAPHS   45

RESEARCH WITH BRAZELTON NEONATAL SCALE
Reliability. Use of scale in infant research. Some conclusions.   48

SUMMARY OF BRAZELTON SCALE SCORING DEFINITIONS   56

EXAMINATION FORM   63

REFERENCES   65

Preface

We are pleased to present this our 50th Clinic in Developmental Medicine. The first Clinic on the neurological examination of the infant by the French school initiated a period, we believe, when doctors have paid far more rigorous attention to the examination of the infant and young child's nervous system. Several further books in our series, notably Prechtl and Beintema's, have developed the vigour of the neurological examination.

The nervous system does not function in a vacuum; it reacts to its environment, and many of our other volumes have looked at this interaction. We think of our Clinics on speech and language, the neuropsychiatric study of childhood, biological factors in temporal lobe epilepsy, and the infant cry.

Over the decade since we began publishing these books, the newborn baby has been studied in innumerable different ways. Alas, too often, while investigative minutiae are being studied, the baby's personality has been ignored. Berry Brazelton's work provides us with the tools to examine the child's behaviour as carefully as we've looked in the past at his neurological system and his biochemistry.

Those who know Dr Brazelton's work will not be surprised that he has provided us with this new and valuable tool for better care of babies and children. Based on deep knowledge as well as empathy with children, his work has always been statistically rigorous as well as original in the ideas that it explores. This book gives us the opportunity for a much broader approach to assessing newborn infants, and by doing so will lead us to be interested in all infants, as well as in those who are sick. In this way Dr Brazelton will help us to improve the quality of the care received and the quality of life for the great majority, instead of giving our efforts too narrowly to an aristocratic minority with rare disorders.

We launch our 50th volume with as much optimism as we launched our first, and we are happy to predict that people will be using and working with it for many years to come.

Martin Bax
Ronald Mac Keith

Foreword

The evaluation of the behaviour of the newborn infant has concerned many who are interested in understanding the relative contribution of the infant to the nature-nurture controversy. In the first half of the twentieth century, emphasis in developmental research was on the environment's effect in shaping the child. In the latter half of this century, the pendulum is swinging. Many researchers feel that the individuality of the infant may be a powerful influence in shaping the outcome of his relationship with his caretakers. Hence there are many reasons for evaluating behavior as early as possible. If Bowlby's (1969) thesis of attachment behavior is as powerful as it seems to be, observations of the neonate and the reactions he engenders in his parents in the early weeks may become the best predictors of the outcome of the mother-father-infant interaction. Thomas *et al.* (1968) have attempted to document the strengths of individual infants' behavior in our culture, and their stability over time for later development. But infants in their studies were first assessed at three months. Neonatal observations of the infants and early assessment of their caretakers might have contributed to our understanding of the relative contributions of each to the interaction. By three months, a great deal of important interaction has already occurred, and future patterns may already be set.

Another example of the importance of early evaluation is that of cross-cultural studies. Differences in groups of neonates (such as those described by Geber and Dean (1959), Cravioto *et al.* (1966), the Freedmans (1969), and Brazelton *et al.* (1969), might identify the kind of neonatal behavior which leads to the perpetuation of child-rearing practices which preserve cross-cultural differences among adults. If we are to understand the ultimate effect of child-rearing practices in a particular group of children, we must see them as infants, and as soon after delivery as possible.

The neonate and his behavior cannot be assumed to be purely of genetic origin. Intrauterine influences are powerful and have already influenced the physiologic and behavioral reactions of the baby at birth. Intrauterine nutrition and infection (Klein *et al.* 1971, Scrimshaw *et al.* 1959, Viteri *et al.* 1964), hormones (Money *et al.* 1968), drugs (Moffeld *et al.* 1968, Brazelton and Robey, 1965), to name a few—are affecting the fetus for nine long months, and there is rapidly accumulating evidence that the newborn is powerfully shaped before delivery. His behavior is phenotypic at birth, not genotypic.

His behavior can be coupled with maternal expectation, based on her past experience with mothering and with infants from her culture, to predict the outcome of their early interaction (Brazelton *et al.* 1971). We must see the relative influence of each on their interaction, and to do this, we must be able to document relative differences in neonatal behavior.

1

Neurologic examinations of infants soon after delivery have culminated in the sensitive, flexible examination of Prechtl and Beintema (1964). This exam has proved its usefulness toward its authors' expressed goals of 'obtaining more exact knowledge of the developing neurological functions as early as possible and of the relationship of obstetrical complications to neurological abnormalities in later life'. The authors emphasize the importance of such an assessment since abnormal signs which are present in the early days or weeks may disappear to be followed months or years later by the appearance of abnormal functions.

The neonatal behavioral and psychologic precursors of abnormal development and of individuality in normal development need to be as clearly documented as do neurological precursors. Neurological examinations (André-Thomas *et al.* 1960, Paine 1960, Prechtl and Beintema 1964) have not been predictive of tremendous variations in normal or even the milder abnormalities of development. I hope that documentation of the wide span of behaviors available to the neonate may reveal some of the precursors for his later personality development. For this purpose, we have developed a behavioral assessment scale. The Neonatal Behavioral Assessment Scale is a psychological scale for the newborn human infant. It allows for an assessment of the infant's capabilities along dimensions that we think are relevant to his developing social relationships.

The baby's state of consciousness is perhaps the single most important element in the behavioural examination. His reactions to all stimulation are dependent upon his ongoing state of consciousness and any interpretation of them must be made with this in mind. In addition, his use of a state to maintain control of his reactions to environmental and internal stimuli is an important mechanism (Brazelton 1961) and reflects his potential for organization. State sets a dynamic pattern which reflects the full behavioral repertoire of the infant. Specifically this examination tracks the pattern of state change over the course of the examination, its lability and its direction in response to external and internal stimuli. Thus, the variability of state becomes a dimension of assessment, pointing to the initial abilities in the infant for self-organization.

Further assessment of the infant's ability for self-organization are contained in the skills measuring his ability for self-quieting after aversive stimuli. This is contrasted to the infant's need for stimuli from the examiner to help him quiet. In the exam, there is a graded series of procedures—talking, hand on belly, restraint, holding and rocking—which are designed to calm the infant. The scale results in an evaluation of the infant's control over interfering motor activity. In addition, the infant's responsiveness to animate—voice and face, cuddling, etc.—and to inanimate stimulation—auditory, e.g. rattle and bell, visual, e.g. red ball and white light, temperature change upon being uncovered, etc.—will be assessed. With these stimuli there is an attempt to elicit the infant's best performance in response to different kinds of stimulation. Other items in the scale include examination of reflexes to assess neurological adequacy and estimates of the vigor and attentional excitement exhibited by the infant.

Implicit to an understanding of the behaviors which we shall attempt to document is a parallel assessment of neurological adequacy (for this we suggest Prechtl and Beintema (1964)), of his maturity at birth (for this refer to Brett (1965) Robinson

(1966) and St. Anne Dargassies (1966)), and of intrauterine conditions of nutrition and/or depletion (dysmaturity scales of Gruenwald (1966), Dubowitz *et al.* (1970), Lubchenko (1970) and Parkin (1971)). Otherwise, neonatal behavior will be seen without understanding the powerful effects of dysfunction resulting from intra-uterine influences.

The behavioral assessment has been used successfully for special groups at risk— such as heavily medicated (Brazelton and Robey 1965), low birth weight, and stressed prematures (Scarr and Williams 1971). This assessment should be accompanied by a detailed pediatric and neurological evaluation. The neonate is making a tremendous physiological readjustment to his extrauterine state, and all of his reactions must be viewed in this context. The fact that he has any energy left over for periods of cognitive or affective responses is the amazing observation. The primacy of his physiological needs results in brief and often unreproducible responses which probably involve the activity of higher nervous system centers. Hence, we have attempted to account for such variability by urging that the scorer assess the neonate's *best* performance— not his average performance. Since we are interested in predicting his eventual capaci-ties as they have been reinforced by physiological recovery and a fostering environ-ment, these periods of *best* performance may be more predictive. The confusion which results from rapidly repeated stimulation which deplete the energy of the fragile organism and demand his protective habituating mechanisms can offer little more than a measure of his available physiological homeostasis. We are interested in more than that.

Repeated tests on several days in the neonatal period are of much more value than any one assessment, for they may depict a curve of recovery and of early develop-ment of the mechanisms which are documented. Just as the neurological examination is best tested as late as possible in the first neonatal period, if but one assessment will be made, the behavioural test may be a more valid predictor of cognitive and social assets after the third day of life. By this time, the overwhelming demands of delivery and early recovery may have decreased, and the neonate's behavior can be seen independent of these powerful external and internal influences.

Although the Apgar scores (Apgar 1960) have proven to have moderate predictive value of the infant's future neurological status, there must be a clinical evaluation which could reflect his future development of a wider range of responses. We would hope that this scale might fill the needs of clinicians and researchers—*viz.* an instrument for assessing the subtler behavioral responses of the neonate as he adjusts to his new environment and gains mastery of his physiological equipment, as he prepares to begin the important period of emotional and cognitive development of infancy. We hope that it will help us understand a caretaker's response to him as we use the assessment scale, and thereby predict the kind of interaction he is likely to set up in his environment.

Introduction

The Brazelton Behavioral Assessment Scale is intended as a means of scoring interactive behavior. It is not a formal neurological evaluation, though the neurological implications of such a scale make it necessary that a few basic neurological items be included. These are based on the descriptions of neurological assessment outlined in Prechtl and Beintema's 'Neurological Examination of the Full Term Infant' (1964). The main thrust of the evaluation is behavioral. It is an attempt to score the infant's available responses to his environment, and so, indirectly, his effect on the environment. It is essentially aimed at evaluating the normal newborn infant, and its use in comparing infants within and across cultures has been demonstrated (Brazelton and Robey 1965, Brazelton *et al.* 1969, Freedman and Freedman 1969, Brazelton *et al.* 1971, Horowitz *et al.* 1971, Scarr and Williams 1971).

The scale has been developed over a number of years with the help of a large number of direct and indirect collaborators. Throughout the period of development, however, one essential thread has been maintained by the extensive clinical pediatric perspective of the senior author. This perspective has imparted characteristics to the assessment procedure which involve an approach somewhat different from standard psychological and neurological tests. The scale differs in ways which require careful consideration by both the traditionally trained pediatrician and the traditionally trained psychologist.

To promote reliability in the scoring, much attention is paid in this manual to the items on the scale in terms of definitions. However, before this specific information on the scale and the items is presented, the following general considerations will be helpful to the potential user.

The scoresheet includes 27 behavioral items, each of which is scored on a nine point scale, and 20 elicited responses, each of which is scored on a three point scale.

Most of the scales are set so that the mid-point is the norm. The mean is related to the expected behavior of an "average" 7 + pound, full term (40 weeks gestation), normal Caucasian infant, whose mother has had not more than 100 mg of barbiturates and 50 mg of other sedative drugs prior to delivery, whose Apgar scores were no less than 7 at 1, 8 at 5 and 8 at 15 minutes after delivery, who needed no special care after delivery, and who had an apparently normal intrauterine experience (i.e. normal hydration, nutrition, color and physiological responses). Since many infants are discoordinated for 48 hours after delivery, the behavior of the third day must be taken as the expected mean. However, this does not mean that the scale cannot be used with younger or disorganized infants. In such cases, the median is still projected as that of a three-day-old, as noted above.

The Brazelton scale departs from many standardized assessment procedures in that, in all but a few items, the infant's score is based on his best, not his average performance. Thus, particularly if the infant has responded poorly or not at all to a particular stimulation, the examiner should make every effort to verify that the subject is not capable of a better response. He should be constantly sensitive to opportunities for repeating tests later in the examination. He should also be aware of maneuvers which could help him elicit the best possible response. Particularly useful are those used by mothers to alert their infants, such as holding, cuddling, rocking and crooning. These are all part of the sensitive examiner's repertoire, as he brings the baby to alert states in order to score the examination.

State

An important consideration throughout the tests is the state of consciousness or 'state' of the infant. Reactions to stimuli must be interpreted within the context of the presenting state of consciousness, as reactions may vary markedly as the infant passes from one state to another. State depends on physiological variables such as hunger, nutrition, degree of hydration, and the time within the wake-sleep cycle of the infant. The pattern of states as well as the movement from one state to another appear to be important characteristics of infants in the neonatal period, and this kind of evaluation may be the best predictor of the infant's receptivity and ability to respond to stimuli in a cognitive sense. Our criteria for determining state are based on our own experiences and on those of others, and are comparable with the descriptions of Prechtl and Beintema (1964). A state is achieved if the child is in the particular state for at least 15 seconds.

Sleep States

(1) Deep sleep with regular breathing, eyes closed, no spontaneous activity except startles or jerky movements at quite regular intervals; external stimuli produce startles with some delay; suppression of startles is rapid, and state changes are less likely than from other states. No eye movements (Fig. 1).

(2) Light sleep with eyes closed; rapid eye movements can be observed under closed lids; low activity level, with random movements and startles or startle equivalents; movements are likely to be smoother and more monitored than in state 1; responds to internal and external stimuli with startle equivalents, often with a resulting change of state. Respirations are irregular, sucking movements occur off and on (Fig. 2).

Awake States

(3) Drowsy or semi-dozing; eyes may be open or closed, eyelids fluttering; activity level variable, with interspersed, mild startles from time to time; reactive to sensory stimuli, but response often delayed; state change after stimulation frequently noted. Movements are usually smooth. Fussing may or may not be present (Figs. 3a & b).

(4) Alert, with bright look; seems to focus attention on source of stimulation, such as an object to be sucked, or a visual or auditory stimulus; impinging stimuli may break through, but with some delay in response. Minimal motor activity (Fig. 4).

(5) Eyes open; considerable motor activity, with thrusting movements of the extremities, and even a few spontaneous startles; reactive to external stimulation with increase in startles or motor activity, but discrete reactions difficult to distinguish because of high activity level. Fussing may or may not be present.

5

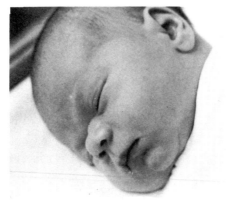 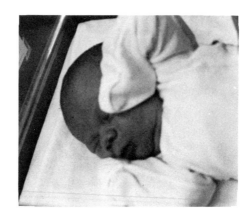

Fig. 1. State 1.   Fig. 2. State 2.

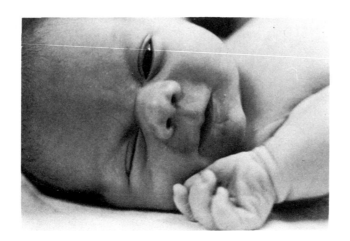

Fig. 3a. State 3.

Fig. 3b. State 3.

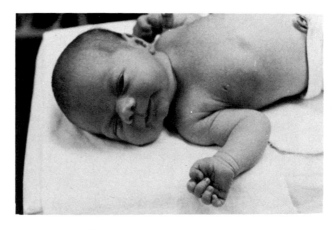

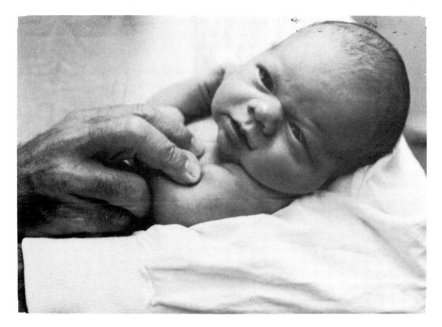

Fig. 4. State 4.

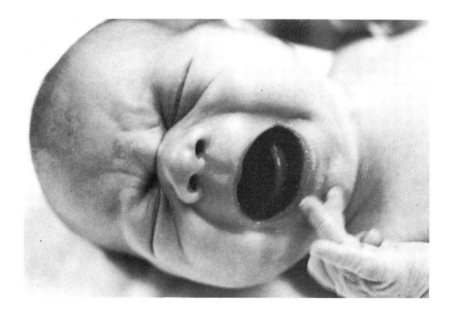

Fig. 5. State 6.

7

(6) Crying; characterized by intense crying which is difficult to break through with stimulation (Fig. 5).

We have suggested in parentheses on the scoring sheet the numbers of the appropriate states in which the assessment of each item on the scale can be made.

Order of Presentation and General Procedure

The assessment of the infant should preferably be carried out in a quiet, dimly-lit room, but, if this is not possible, disturbing aspects of a noisy, brightly-lit room must be noted as part of the stimulation to which the infant might be reacting.

The examination itself usually takes between 20 and 30 minutes, and involves about 30 different tests and maneuvers. These should be performed in the following order:*

Observe infant for two minutes—note state
Flashlight (3 to 10 times) through closed lids
Rattle (3 to 10 times)
Bell (3 to 10 times)
Uncover infant
Light pin-prick (5 times)
Ankle clonus
Plantar grasp
Babinski response
Undress infant
Passive movements and general tone
Orientation, inanimate: visual and auditory
Palmar grasp
Pull to sit
Standing
Walking
Placing
Incurvation
Body tone across hand
Crawling—prone responses
Pick up and hold
Glabella reflex
Spin—tonic deviation and reflex
Orientation, animate: visual, auditory, and visual and auditory
Cloth on face
Tonic neck response
Moro response

The items on the scale are scored according to the infant's reactions and responses to these maneuvers and tests. Some items are scored according to the infant's response

---

*The reader may like to look at this in relationship to the scoring sheet which is printed on pages 63, 64 and also in the slip case inside the back cover.

to specific stimuli; others, such as consolability (item 16) and alertness (item 10) are a result of continuous behavioral observations throughout the assessment.

The examination should begin with the infant asleep, covered and dressed, about mid-way between two feedings. It is preferable that he be examined in a quiet, semi-darkened room with a temperature of 72°-80°F. After an assessment of his initial state, stimuli which can be offered discretely (*i.e.* auditory and visual) are presented.

Thus, while the infant is still in the wrapped, quiet situation (state 1, 2 or 3), the flashlight is produced (Fig. 6), and the degree of response and the response decrement to repeated flashes is noted. Next the response decrement to repeated auditory stimuli is assessed, using first the rattle, and then, unless the infant has come to an alert state, the bell. Often, after the above stimuli have been presented, the infant will begin to rouse. He should then be uncovered, and any relevant reactions to this change recorded (*e.g.* lability of skin color, rapidity of build up from quiet to agitated state). Since the scale scores his *best* performance, any maneuver which brings out his best performance should be utilized and noted.

Fig. 6. Equipment needed as stimuli.

While the infant is still quiet (*i.e.* in state 1, 2 or 3), the examiner should test for response decrement to a light pin-prick. He should note how totally and how rapidly the whole body responds, and how rapidly the infant is able to shut down this response to subsequent pricks. Meanwhile, an assessment should be made of the speed of state change, as the infant moves to 'wide-awake' state. Then, with the infant still dressed, clonus (ankle), foot grasp and Babinski response should be determined. The assessment of his passive motor tone could be very disturbing if it were performed too vigorously. This is not necessary, and it is preferable to have a cooperative baby. All maneuvers should be performed with an eye to producing the neonate's *best* performance. Sensitivity to him is necessary to do this.

Once the infant has come to an awake-alert state, the examiner is free to vary the order of administration of items to take maximum advantage of the infant's state and readiness to respond at a particular moment. Thus, while orientation items come twenty-fourth in the above list, the examiner should try some of them as soon as the infant is awake, alert and not crying (*i.e.* before testing 'pull-to-sit' or prone behavior (twentieth). There are however a few constraints on this flexibility. The stimuli classified as aversive* must be administered in the given order, within the framework

---

*There are four maneuvers which are considered moderately aversive: uncovering, undressing, being pulled to sit, and being placed in prone. In addition, four are considered to be strongly aversive: pin-prick, elicitation of the tonic neck reflex, elicitation of the Moro reflex, and elicitation of defensive reactions (cloth on face).

of the exam. Also, 'pull-to-sit' should always be executed before testing of the disturbing elicited reflexes.

As the infant moves to wide-awake alertness, he may be undressed. Once again, he should be observed for state change, lability of skin color, speed of build up, etc. in response to this disturbing maneuver. General tone is assessed as he is handled, and when he is first undressed. Passive movements are also graded at this point, while he is wake and alert, but not disturbed. Testing for orientation response to visual and auditory inanimate stimuli (items 5 and 6 of scale) should follow. The infant is rated according to his ability to fix on a bright object and follow it with his eyes, and the degree of orientation an auditory stimulus (such as a soft ball) held out of sight.

So long as he remains in an awake state, the infant can also be pulled to sit. Standing, walking and placing reflexes follow easily. Next, incurvation, body tone across the examiner's hand and prone responses are assessed. The infant should then be picked up and held, and spun round slowly for vestibular responses and nystagmus (for description of these maneuvers refer to the work of Prechtl and Beintema (1964)). At this point it should be possible to test for orientation responses to animate stimuli (items 7, 8 and 9 of scale). Finally, the response to the cloth-on-face maneuver, the tonic neck reflex, and the Moro reflex are tested. Since these maneuvers are disturbing, they provide an excellent opportunity for assessing the infant's self-quieting behavior and his consolability.

At any point during the examination when the infant becomes upset, the examiner should wait 15 seconds before attempting comforting procedures, so that the subject has an opportunity to quiet himself; any self-quieting behavior which occurs should be carefully observed. If no self-quieting occurs, the infant should be comforted, using the following procedures in order: (1) examiner's face; (2) face and voice; (3) hand on belly; (4) restraining one arm; (5) restraining both arms; (6) holding him; (7) holding and rocking him; (8) holding, rocking, and talking to him. The infant's consolability is assessed according to how many of these graded procedures prove necessary to quiet him.

Such measures as hand-to-mouth facility, tremulousness, amount of startle, vigor and activity are continuously assessed. In addition, the examiner must count the number of state changes which occur throughout the exam. Some examiners find that clicking a small mechanical counter aids their accuracy in doing this.

It is important that the examiner should attempt to bring the baby through an *entire spectrum* of states in each examination. Ideally, one would like to see the infant perform in each state, so that his capacity to handle states and his responses in each one can be assessed. In order to bring him through this state spectrum, the examiner should attempt to alert the infant gradually without upsetting him, and it is for this reason that the aversive stimuli are graded and presented in a particular order (see page 35).

Finally, a record is made on the scoresheet of the infant's weight loss and weight recovery. These measurements are important in assessing the state of hydration and electrolyte balance.

Not more than two infants should be assessed in one half day without a rest, since the examiner's fatigue will interfere with his accuracy.

Scoring

Except for the first few items which can be scored immediately, the majority of items are scored at the end of the examination. Scoring usually takes about 15 minutes. As has already been noted, the infant is scored on most items for his best performance. We have found it advisable to make notes during the exam on certain items—e.g. state changes, startles, hand to mouth, color changes, rapidity of buildup, irritability. Otherwise, reliability is difficult to maintain.

The score sheet itself has been designed to provide a compact and easily utilized record. For the 27 major items, scored on a nine-point scale, a check mark is made in the appropriate box. On a few items, such as motor maturity, the infant's behavior may show distinct variations from one period of the exam to another. Under such circumstances, the examiner may wish to use a supplementary score to indicate that the infant has shown behavior very different from that rated as his best performance. This secondary score should be indicated with a circle or other consistent mark. However, in general, the use of secondary scores is not recommended, although for individual studies this practice may prove useful.

A nine point scale has been used, and each point carefully documented in order that examiners can reach high agreement on each item. A nine point scale allows for a range of behaviors which can bring out subtle differences among different groups of babies. For example, cross cultural differences may not appear unless the range of behavior is great enough to allow for very slight but definite differences among groups of infants. The scale is also being used to assess groups of immature and small-for-dates infants. Much of their behavior will cluster in one half of the possible scores for each item. Having a range for immature babies increases the scale's sensitivity to individual differences among a group of infants who are restricted in their responses. Important variations in behavior can still be recorded. If we started with an overall three or five point scale, the sensitivity of each item to important individual differences of these kinds would be markedly diminished. However, having a nine point scale makes for some overlapping in scoring from point to point in average neonates on some items. Hence, we have used only two point differences as our criterion for non-agreement. In this way, we can subsume examiners' differences in scoring apparent, overlapping observations.

As the reader will soon realize, some items are optimal at the midpoint (a score of 5), whereas others are optimal at a score of 9. There has been no attempt to create a scale whose summary score can be interpreted as 'optimal' behavior in the neonate. The author believes there is no such thing as 'optimal neonatal behavior', since for each baby optimal behavior may be represented by an entirely different cluster of scores. If any attempt must be made to use total scores to reflect 'optimal' or 'poor' functioning, it must be done with clusters of items, and reflect the 'optimal' within each individual group. A series of correlation coefficients might do this for any given population, but to generalize beyond that would be absurd in the light of present information about the predictive meaning of neonatal behavior.

The 20 elicited reflexes are scored as follows: X = not done; O = not elicited; L = 1 = low; M = 2 = medium; and H = 3 = high. In addition, any asymmetry (A) should be carefully noted. Eighty per cent of babies will score a 2. The technique of eliciting these responses is not described in this manual. In general we follow method outlined by Prechtl and Beintema (1964).

Finally, the section headed 'Descriptive Paragraph' should be completed. This involves the scoring of a few subjective items, and the writing of a short descriptive paragraph giving further comments and information which might be considered relevant to the assessment.

Examiner Training

This manual is intended as an introduction to the Brazelton Behavioral Assessment Scale, and as a constant guide to the trained examiner. It is not intended as a substitute for direct training. Both those naive and inexperienced in the handling of infants require direct training in the administration and scoring of the scale. As noted by Horowitz *et al.* (1971), a naive examiner can be trained to high independent inter-scorer reliability (0.85-0.90) in the course of testing ten infants. Individuals with extensive infant experience may be able to achieve reliability in a shorter amount of time. A list of trained examiners who can provide training can be obtained by writing to the senior author. There are four training films which are available to be used with the manual. These can be obtained by writing to Educational Development Corporation, 8 Mifflin Place, Cambridge, Mass. 02138.*

*These training films have been made with the aid of a grant from the Grant Foundation.

The Manual

State Observations

Since an infant's reactions will be state-related, it is vital that observations on his 'state' should be considered as a starting point from which all other observations are made. An infant's use of states as a framework for his reactions to the examiner may be most important as a part of the observation.

Initial State

In the two minutes before stimulation is begun, an assessment of the infant's state is made by observing his spontaneous behavior, respirations (assessed from the movement of the gown or covering sheet), eye movements, startles, and responses to concurrent spontaneous events in the environment. States are scored according to the criteria set out on page 5.

Predominant States

At the end of the examination period, the examiner should record the two or at the most three predominant states within which the infant has performed. Since the most important influence on the infant's scores will be his available states, it is important to have an idea of the range and variety of states used by him in this period, their importance to him in controlling himself, and the amount of time spent in each one.

Response Decrement to Light

(STATE 1, 2 OR 3)

One of the most impressive mechanisms in the neonate is his capacity to decrease responses to repeated disturbing stimuli (Fig. 7 a & b). In this test, an attempt is made to measure the decrement which occurs in a quiet state (2 or 3), after the infant has responded with an aversive reaction to a flashlight shone briefly in his eyes (closed or open). Since some babies will alert as the flashlight is shone on them, they will show no obvious aversive reaction. When this happens, the infant should be allowed to alert himself, and after he begins to respond with an aversive reaction (tight blinking, general motor activity and change in respiration) habituation should be measured by noting any real decrement in the extent of these reactions. If he sleeps too deeply, the crib can be shaken gently or he can be uncovered gently in order to rouse him for an observable response. Otherwise, decrement cannot be observed.

13

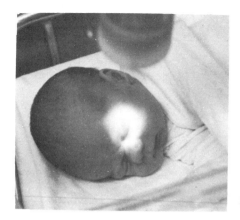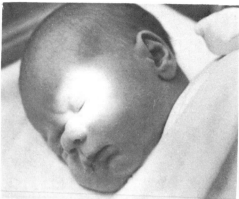

Figs. 7a (*left*) **and 7b** (*right*). Blink reaction to light.

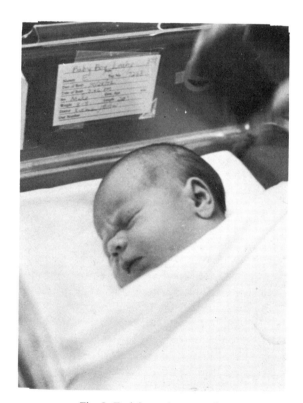

Fig. 8. Facial reaction to rattle.

14

Up to ten stimuli can be used. The passing of two trials without response is taken as the criterion for assessing 'shut-down'. The score given should reflect the stimulus at which greatest degree of response decrement was last observed. Stimuli should be presented approximately five seconds after the end of the previous response. This implies the observer's ability to judge the end of each reaction.

This test should be carried out using a standard eight inch flashlight with two medium-sized batteries in good working condition. Since a baby will, of course, respond differently in a semi-darkened, quiet room than in a brightly-lit, noisy nursery, any ambient noise should be accounted for, and, where possible, ruled out, although the ideal of a quiet, darkened room cannot always be achieved.

The response decrement over time is assessed on the basis of the neonate's ability to control the following reactions: (1) all or none startles of the entire body; (2) delayed and graded localized startle; (3) respiratory changes; (4) blinks of the eyelids. The delaying and finally the suppression of any reactions are degrees of the same kind of habituation. The infant's performance is evaluated after ten flashes, unless he has successfully shut down his response before that.

If there is never any response, score him NA.

Scoring

1 No diminution in high responses over 10 stimuli.

2 Startles delayed; rest of responses still present (*i.e.* body movement, eye blinks, and respiratory changes continue over 10 trials).

3 No startles; other responses, including body movement, still present after 10 trials.

4 No startles; body movement delayed; respiratory changes and blinks continue unchanged over 10 trials.

5 Shutdown of bodymovements; some diminution in blinks and respiratory changes after 9-10 stimuli.

6 Shutdown of body movements; some diminution in blinks and respiratory changes after 7-8 stimuli.

7 Shutdown of body movements; some diminution in blinks and respiratory changes after 5-6 stimuli.

8 Shutdown of body movements; some diminution in blinks and respiratory changes after 3-4 stimuli.

9 Shutdown of body movements; some diminution in blinks and respiratory changes after 1-2 stimuli.

Response Decrement to Rattle

(STATES 1, 2 AND 3)

Response Decrement to Bell

(STATES 1, 2 AND 3)

These items are designed to measure the neonates' ability to shut out a disturbing auditory stimulus (Fig. 8). Hence, (as in item 1) the stimulus must be able to break through the ambient conditions and create a startle response. The bell may be more successful in doing this, especially in a noisy nursery. Often, the rattle may bring the baby out of his generally shut-down state, in which case testing should be continued with the bell. The bell should be similar to the one used in a standard Gesell Test.

The infant is scored (as above) according to his ability to delay and shut down his aversive reactions (general startle, tight blinking and respiratory changes) as he habituates himself to repeated stimuli. Even a temporary suppression of these reactions is evidence of his ability to shut out the disturbing stimuli. If the baby is too sleepy to show any response, he can be roused slightly by shaking the bed or uncovering him. If he never makes any response score him NA.

These tests should be carried out only while the infant is in state 1, 2 or 3. The stimuli should be brief and discrete. Each one should be presented five seconds after the end of the response to the previous one. The test should continue until the infant has made no response to two consecutive stimuli, or until ten stimuli have been presented. The procedure should be performed first with the rattle and then with the bell.

Scoring

1 No diminution in high responses over 10 stimuli.
2 Startles delayed; rest of responses still present (*i.e.* body movements, eye blinks and respiratory changes continue over 10 trials).
3 Startles no longer present but rest are still present, including body movement in 10 trials.
4 No startles, body movement delayed, respiratory and blinks same in 10 trials.
5 Shutdown of body movements, some diminution in blinks and respiratory changes in 9-10 stimuli.
6 .. in 7-8 stimuli.
7 .. in 5-6 stimuli.
8 .. in 3-4 stimuli.
9 .. in 1-2 stimuli.

Response Decrement to Pinprick

As a test of response decrement to tactile stimulation, the diaper pin may be used to prick the heel of the infant's foot when he is quiet (Fig. 9a, b & c). This may be repeated several times. The examiner watches for how totally and how rapidly the whole body responds to this pinprick. In an immature or CNS-damaged infant, the opposite foot withdraws and the whole body responds as quickly as the stimulated foot (a demonstration of the all-or-none aspect of an immature organism). The degree, rapidity, and repetition of this 'spread' of stimulus to the rest of the body is measured here. The other aspect is the infant's capacity to shut down this spread of a generalized response. When he continues to respond in an obligatory, repetitive way, he rates a low score. As he demonstrates a suppression of responses to the stimulus and changes his state to a more alert, receptive one, he deserves a high score. Many infants demonstrate some but not all of this behavior, and it may be evidence of excellent CNS function. Middle scores are saved for infants who demonstrate some habituation but not an accompanying state change to alertness.

The foot should be pricked at least four times. If no response decrement occurs, the stimulation should be stopped. If decrement occurs, a fifth stimulus and more can be applied to test the extent of the decrement. (An appropriate stimulus is a pin pushed through a cork to extend 1/16th of an inch beyond the cork.)

Scoring

1 Response generalized to whole body and increases over trials.

2 Both feet withdraw together. No decrement of response.

3 Variable response to stimulus. Response decrement but return of response.

4 Response decrement after five trials. Localized to stimulated leg. No change to alert state.

5 Response decrement after five trials. Localized to stimulated foot. No change to alert state.

6 Response limited to stimulated foot after 3-4 trials. No change to alert state.

7 Response limited to stimulated foot after 1-2 trials. No change to alert state.

8 Response localized and minimal. Change to alert state (4).

9 Complete response decrement. Change to alert state (4).

NA No response, hence no decrement.

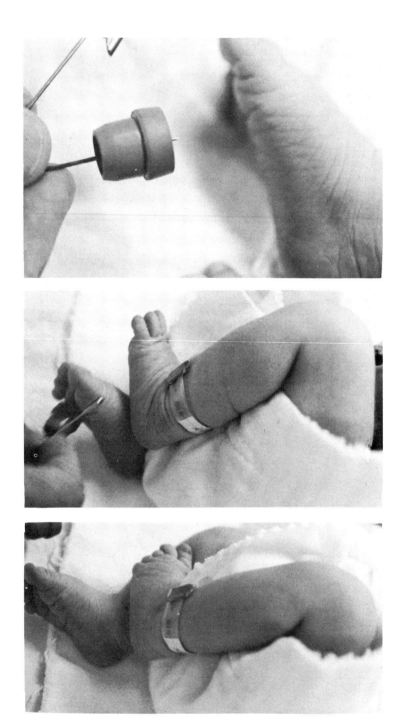

Figs. 9a (*top*), **9b** (*center*) **and 9c** (*bottom*). The pinprick to sole of foot, with withdrawal of other leg.

18

Orientation Response - Inanimate Visual

Since most neonates will demonstrate some ability to fix on a visual object (a contrasting bright or shiny object, *e.g.*, a bell, red ball, white mask) and follow it horizontally for brief excursions, this is a measure of that ability (Fig. 10). It is highly state-related, and may not be demonstrated in any one exam, but, under optimal conditions (a quiet, semi-dark room), it is repeatable; following with the eyes is also accompanied by headturning to follow. Vertical following seems of an even higher order, and many babies will stretch their necks to follow up and down (Fig. 11a & b). This becomes a summary score.

The infant may respond with (1) alerting (decrease in random activity, focus on the object when it is in his line of vision, slow regular respirations, and follows when it moves in arcs) and (2) brightening (change in facial expression. widening of eyes and brighter look, jagged respirations, with an associated decrease in random activity) (Fig. 12).

When the infant will not attend or follow in the bassinet, he may be held on the E's lap, slightly propped up (Fig. 13a and b). This facilitates his doll's eye reflex; his eyes open, and he attends to the object. Obviously, the act of holding him restrains interfering movement and helps alert him. But he may also be distracted by the examiner's face. Held at the E's shoulder, his following responses can be determined by another examiner.

Scoring

1 Does not focus on or follow stimulus.

2 Stills with stimulus and brightens.

3 Stills, focuses on stimulus when presented, little spontaneous interest, brief following.

4 Stills, focuses on stimulus, follows for 30° arc, jerky movements.

5 Focuses and follows with eyes horizontally for at least a 30° arc. Smooth movement, loses stimulus but finds it again.

6 Follows for 30° arcs with eyes and head. Eye movements are smooth.

7 Follows with eyes and head at least 60° horizontally, maybe briefly vertically, partly continuous movement, loses stimulus occasionally, head turns to follow.

8 Follows with eyes and head 60° horizontally and 30° vertically.

9 Focuses on stimulus and follows with smooth, continuous head movement horizontally, vertically, and in a circle. Follows for 120° arc.

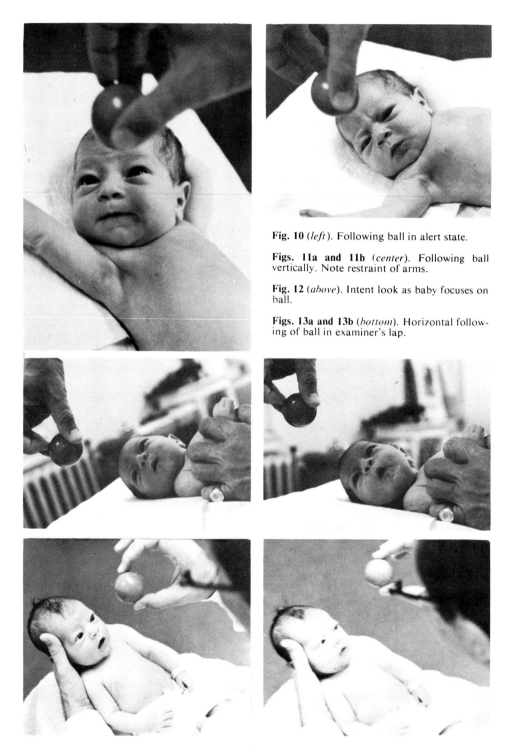

Fig. 10 (*left*). Following ball in alert state.

Figs. 11a and 11b (*center*). Following ball vertically. Note restraint of arms.

Fig. 12 (*above*). Intent look as baby focuses on ball.

Figs. 13a and 13b (*bottom*). Horizontal following of ball in examiner's lap.

20

Orientation Response - Inanimate Auditory

This is a measure of his response to the rattle or a soft bell as a (non-social) stimulus when he is in an alert state (Fig. 14). The auditory stimuli should be presented to each side and out of sight (at least 6″ away and no more than 12″) so that one can observe the infant's eyes and head as they respond to the lateralized stimulus. This scores his best performance in one of the awake states to the stimulus. Alerting eye shift and head turning to the stimulus are scored. Brightening of face and eyes can be seen, and they are evidences of his attention to the stimulus. If an observable response does not occur on the first presentation, it may be repeated later. Do not use a pure tone, but a mixed one as produced by a simple rattle.

Scoring

1   No reaction.
2   Respiratory change or blink only.
3   General quieting as well as blink and respiratory changes.
4   Stills, brightens, no attempt to locate source.
5   Shifting of eyes to sound, as well as stills and brightens.
6   Alerting and shifting of eyes and head turn to source.
7   Alerting, head turns to stimulus, and search with eyes.
8   Alerting prolonged, head and eyes turn to stimulus repeatedly.
9   Turning and alerting to stimulus presented on both sides on every presentation of stimulus.

Orientation - Animate Visual

The next three items score the attention which is called up by the examiner's social cues—voice, face, cuddling, holding, rocking, etc. The infant may respond with alerting, brightening, and settling into the arms (Fig. 15a & b). He may turn his head to seek the face. Having caught the examiner he may rivet his attention, and 'lock' on for long periods (Fig. 16). No interest is unusual. How he is held may strongly influence this, and the E should attempt to reproduce two maneuvers commonly used by mothers: (1) hold the infant in a cuddled position in the arms up against the chest, and (2) upright on the shoulder.

For the 'visual only' item the examiner places his face in the baby's line of vision then moves it slowly in lateral and vertical arcs until the baby stops following.

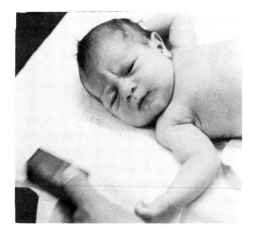

Fig. 14. Head-turning to rattle.

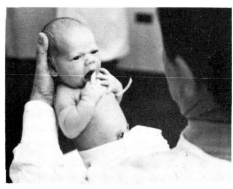

Fig. 15a. Orientation and head-turning to face.

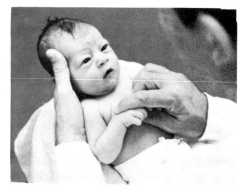

Fig. 15b. Orientation to face and brightening.

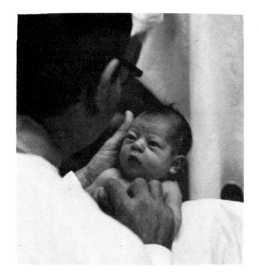

Fig. 16. Intense attention (brightening) to face.

Scoring

1 Does not focus on or follow stimulus.

2 Stills with stimulus and brightens.

3 Stills, focuses on stimulus when presented, brief following.

4 Stills, focuses on stimulus, follows for 30° arc, jerky movements.

5 Focuses and follows with eyes horizontally for at least a 30° arc. Smooth movement, loses stimulus but finds it again.

6 Follows for 30° arcs with eyes and with head. Eye movements are smooth.

7 Follows with eyes and head at least 60° horizontally, maybe briefly vertically, partly continuous movement, loses stimulus occasionally, head turns to follow.

8 Follows with eyes and head 60° horizontally and 30° vertically.

9 Focuses on stimulus and follows with smooth, continuous head movement horizontally, vertically, and in a circle. Follows for 120° arc.

Orientation - Animate Auditory

(STATES 4 AND 5)

The examiner removes his face from infant's line of sight and talks to him from one side (6 to 12 inches from ear). Continuous, soft and high-pitched speech is the best stimulus, *e.g.* infant's own name.

Scoring

1 No reaction.

2 Respiratory change or blink only.

3 General quieting as well as blink and respiratory changes.

4 Stills, brightens, no attempt to locate source.

5 Shifting of eyes to sound, as well as stills and brightens.

6 Alerting and shifting of eyes and head turn to source.

7 Alerting, head turns to stimulus, and search with eyes.

8 Alerting prolonged, head and eyes turn to stimulus repeatedly.

9 Turning and alerting to stimulus presented on both sides on every presentation of stimulus.

Orientation Animate - Visual and Auditory

The same criteria for scoring are used as in Items 5 and 7. The same conditions pertain except that the examiner's voice is used to reinforce face, both on the bed and when infant is held. The voice is continuous while the face is moving (Fig. 17).

Scoring

1   Does not focus on or follow stimulus.

2   Stills with stimulus and brightens.

3   Stills, focuses on stimulus when presented, brief following.

4   Stills, focuses on stimulus, follows for 30° arc, jerky movements.

5   Focuses and follows with eyes horizontally and/or vertically for at least a 30° arc. Smooth movement, loses stimulus but finds it again.

6   Follows for 30° arcs, with eyes and head. Eye movements are smooth.

7   Follows with eyes and head at least 60° horizontally, maybe briefly vertically, partially continuous movement, loses stimulus occasionally, head turns to follow.

8   Follows with eyes and head 60° horizontally and 30° vertically.

9   Focuses on stimulus and follows with smooth, continuous head movement horizontally, vertically, and in a circle. Follows for at least a 120° arc.

Alertness

This assesses the frequency of the *best periods of* alertness as shown by his responsivity to the E within these best periods. These periods can occur at any time during the exam period. Often this is elicited while the E holds the infant. Since newborns are as variable as they are, and are alert for such a short period, one must assume that any period of alertness in a 30 minute exam may be taken as an index of the infant's 'capacity for responsiveness'. In a less randomly selected time sample than this, or when one can wait for a spontaneous period of alertness, this measure might be a better index of his accessibility but I have found that most infants show small periods of alert behavior during an exam. These should be assessed. Alerting is defined as brightening and widening of eyes, while orienting is used for the response of turning toward the direction of stimulation (Fig. 18).

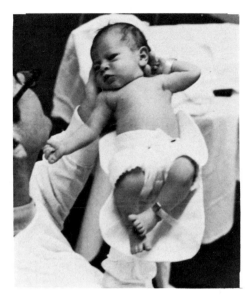

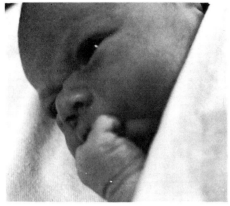

Fig. 18. Alertness.

Fig. 17. Head-turning to voice and face.

Scoring

1 Inattentive—rarely or never responsive to direct stimulation.

2 When alert responsivity brief and generally quite delayed—alerting and orientation very brief and general. Not specific to stimuli.

3 When alert responsibity brief and somewhat delayed—quality of alertness variable.

4 When alert, responsivity somewhat brief but not generally delayed though variable.

5 When alert, responsivity of moderate duration and response generally not delayed and less variable.

6 When alert, responsivity moderately sustained and not delayed. May use stimulation to come to alert state.

7 When alert, episodes are of generally sustained duration, etc.

8 Always has sustained periods of alertness in best periods. Alerting and orientation frequent and reliable. Stimulation brings infant to alert state and quiets infant.

9 Always alert in best periods. Stimulation always elicits alerting, orienting. Infant reliably uses stimulation to quiet self or maintain quiet state.

25

General Tone - Predominant Tone

This scores the motor tone of the baby in his most characteristic states of responsiveness. Since this is a summary assessment, it should include the overall tone as he responds to being handled. This should be assessed in state 4—unless there is no opportunity to produce such an assessment. This should not be assessed in 6.

Strictly, tone means the resistance of parts of the body to passive movement. In the child even more than in the adult the posture reflects tone to a large extent. Positioning the baby allows gravity to impose a passive force on the child's body. The floppy baby will therefore be like a rag doll in both ventral and supine suspension. In the baby, when the tone is increased, the baby holds his limbs in flexed postures and it is in attempting to break these postures either with gravity or by passive movement that the observer notes increased tone.

Tone becomes a summary assessment of motor responses as evaluated when he is at rest and is confirmed by handling and testing his motor resistance when handled. Tone is assessed in such maneuvers as spontaneous activity, pull to sit, holding him over hand horizontally, prone placement, etc., and should be an overall assessment of his body tone as he reacts to all of these.

Scoring

1 Flaccid, limp like a ragdoll, no resistance when limbs are moved, complete head lag in pull to sit.

2 Little response felt as he is moved, but less than about 25% of the time.

3 Flaccid, limp most of the time, but is responsive about 25% of the time with some tone.

4 Some tone half the time, responds to being handled with average tone less than half the time.

5 Tone average when handled, lies in fairly flaccid state in between handling.

6 Variable tone in resting, responsive with good tone as he is handled approximately 75% of the time.

7 Is on the hypertonic side approximately 50% of the time.

8 When handled he is responsive with hypertonicity about 75% of the time.

9 Hypertonic at rest (in flexion) and hypertonic all the time (abnormal).

Motor Maturity

Motor maturity is demonstrated by smooth movements of the extremities and a free, wide range of movements. This is a measure of motor responses—spontaneous

26

and elicited—assessed throughout the exam in the alert states. The arm movements are the easiest to score. The assessment is of (1) smoothness versus jerkiness which reflects the balanced flexor and extensors versus the unbalanced cogwheel movement of short gestation or with possible irritation of the central nervous system. In these babies the flexors and extensors seem to be competing, and (2) freedom of arcs of movement (45-90°) versus restricted arcs (45° or less) (arms and legs in flexion). The short gestation baby has unlimited freedom of movement (floppy) in lateral, sagittal, and cephalad areas, but the movements are jerky and cog-like, overshooting their marks. The very mature infant has both freedom of movement in all directions associated with a smooth, balanced performance (not floppy). The average newborn is somewhat limited in arcs of movement—especially those above the head, and somewhat in the lateral plane.

Scoring

1   Cogwheel-like jerkiness, overshooting of legs and arms in all directions.

2   Jerky movements and mild overshooting.

3   Jerky movements, no overshooting.

4   Only occasional jerky movements predominating arcs to 45°.

5   Smooth movements predominate, arcs predominately 60° half the time.

6   Smooth movements, arcs predominately 60°.

7   Smooth movements and arcs of 90° less than half of the time.

8   Smooth movements and unrestricted arms laterally 90° most of the time.

9   Smoothness, unrestricted (90°) all of the time.

Pull-to-sit

(STATES 3, 4 AND 5)

The examiner places a forefinger in each of the infant's palms. With the arms extended, the infant's automatic grasp is used to pull him to sit. The shoulder girdle muscles respond with tone, and muscular resistance to stretching his neck and lower musculature as he is pulled into a sitting position. Usually he will also attempt to right his head into a position which is in the midline of his trunk and parallel to his body. Since his head is heavy and out of proportion to the rest of his body mass, this is not usually possible and his head falls backward as he comes up. In a seated position, he attempts to right his head, and it may fall forward. Several attempts to right it can be felt via the shoulder muscles as the examiner maintains his grasp on the infant's arms. A few infants make no attempt at all (Fig. 19 a, b, c, d & e).

27

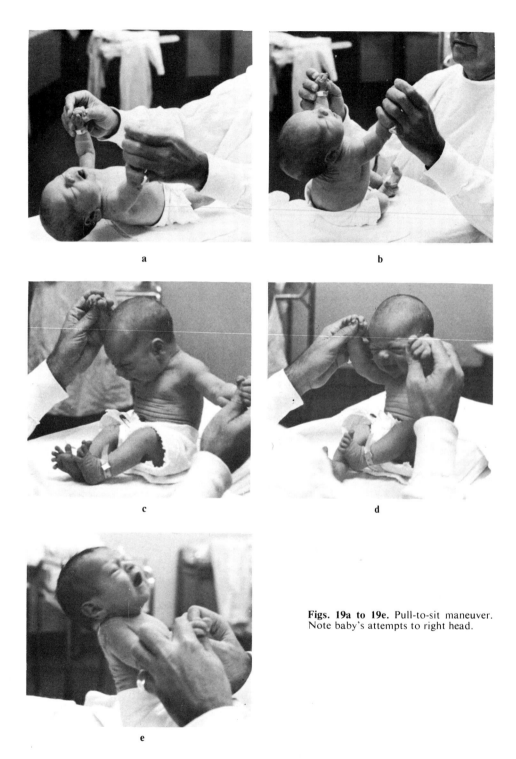

a

b

c

d

e

Figs. 19a to 19e. Pull-to-sit maneuver. Note baby's attempts to right head.

28

Some infants resist flexion and head righting by arching backward. This must be overcome before he can be scored. The average infant makes one or two attempts to maintain his head in an upright position after he is seated, and can participate as he is brought to sit. This should be scored when he is awake enough to participate (states 3 to 5), and is scored on his best performance.

Scoring

1   Head flops completely in pull to sit, no attempts to right it in sitting.

2   Futile attempts to right head but some shoulder tone increase is felt.

3   Slight increase in shoulder tone, seating brings head up once but not maintained, no further efforts.

4   Shoulder and arm tone increase, seating brings head up, not maintained but there are further efforts to right it.

5   Head and shoulder tone increase as pulled to sit, brings head up once to midline by self as well, maintains it for 1-2 seconds.

6   Head brought up twice after seated, shoulder tone increase as comes to sit, and maintained for more than 2 seconds.

7   Shoulder tone increase but head not maintained until seated, then can keep it in position 10 seconds.

8   Excellent shoulder tone, head up while brought up but cannot maintain without falling, repeatedly rights it.

9   Head up during lift and maintained for one minute after seated, shoulder girdle and whole body tone increases as pulled to sit.

Cuddliness

(STATES 4 AND 5)

This is a measure of the infant's response to being held. There are several components which are scored in summary of his responses to being held in a cuddled position against the examiner's chest, and up on his shoulder. The responses are a measure of his negative, or positive responses, as well as none at all.

Scoring

1   Actually resists being held, continuously pushing away, thrashing or stiffening.

2   Resists being held most but not all of the time.

3   Doesn't resist but doesn't participate either, lies passively in arms and against shoulder (like a sack of meal).

4 Eventually molds into arms, but after a lot of nestling and cuddling by examiner.

5 Usually moulds and relaxes when first held, i.e., nestles head in crook of neck and of elbow of examiner. Turns toward body when held horizontally, on shoulder he seems to lean forward.

6 Always moulds initially with above activity.

7 Always moulds initially with nestling, and turning toward body, and leaning forward.

8 In addition to moulding and relaxing, he nestles and turns head, leans forward on shoulder, fits feet into cavity of other arm, all of body participates.

9 All of the above, and baby grasps hold of the examiner to cling to him.

Defensive Movements

(STATES 3, 4 AND 5)

A small cloth is placed with examiner's fingers asserting light pressure over the upper part of the face which would partially occlude the nose, and is kept in place for one minute, or until the infant responds with a series of responses: (1) general quieting (b) mouthing (c) head turning and rooting from side to side (d) head turning laterally as well as neck stretching up and down (e) general undirected increase in activity (f) directed swipes in general area of cloth (g) directed swipes in specific area of cloth which removes the cloth. Infant's hands should not be under cloth (Fig. 20 a, b, c, d & e).

Scoring

  1 No response.

  2 General quieting.

  3 Nonspecific activity increase with long latency.

  4 Same with short latency.

  5 Rooting and lateral head turning.

  6 Neck stretching.

  7 Nondirected swipes of arms.

  8 Directed swipes of arms.

  9 Successful removal of cloth with swipes.

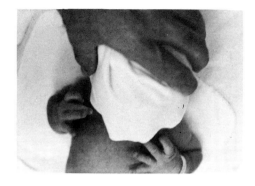

a

b

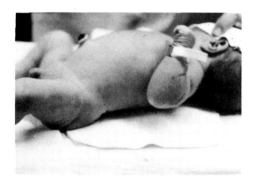

c

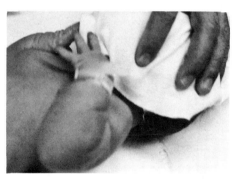

d

Figs. 20a to 20e. Defensive reactions to cloth on face. Picture (c) shows baby twisting head, (d) shows him bringing hands up to face, and (e) shows him turning head and effecting directed swipes. We normally only cover the infant's eyes and not the nose.

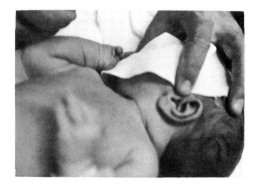

e

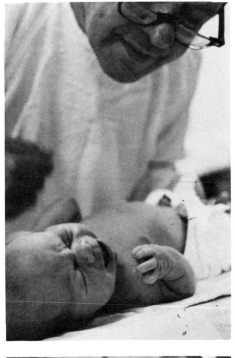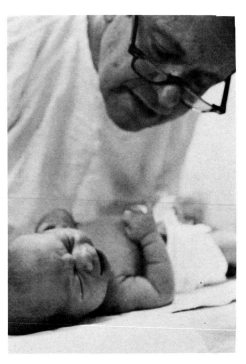

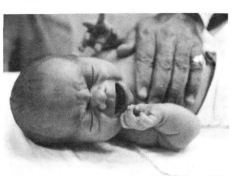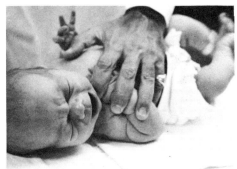

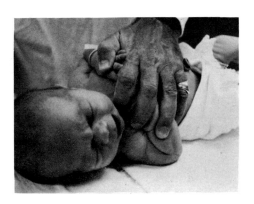

Figs. 21a to 21f. Consoling: (a) (*top left*) presenting face alone; (b) (*top right*) face and voice; (c) (*center left*) hand placed steadily on belly; (d) (*center right*) containing one arm with hand; (e) (*left*) containing both arms with hand; (f) (*facing page—left*) picking up and rocking; (g) (*facing page—right*) holding and rocking—baby finally quiets.

32

Consolability with Intervention

This is measured in an upset state after the infant has been actively fussing or crying for 15 seconds. If he never becomes that upset, it must be scored NA. This measures the number of activities on the part of E which are necessary to interfere with this fussing state and allow the baby to move to a quieter state. Some infants will quiet only when they are dressed and left alone. Any stimulus from the environment disturbs them. Others will quiet when they are held and actively rocked. A steady hand held on a crying baby's belly will act as a soothing stimulus. Others need one or both arms held in addition to the hand on the belly. Holding the arm or arms interferes with the disturbing startle activity which gets triggered off by crying or fussing. A few babies may quiet to the E's voice or face. Consoling is demonstrated when baby quiets for at least five seconds. The activities used to console the infant are graded in reverse order, and best performance is scored (Fig. 21 a-g).

Scoring

1 Not consolable.
2 Pacifier or finger to suck in addition to dressing, holding and rocking.
3 Dressing, holding in arms and rocking.
4 Holding and rocking.
5 Picking up and holding.
6 Hand on belly and restraining one or both arms.
7 Hand on belly steadily.
8 Examiner's voice and face alone.
9 Examiner's face alone.

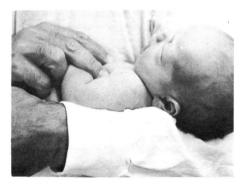 

(*Fig. 21 contd.*)

Peak of Excitement

This is a measure of the overall amount of motor and crying activity observed by the examiner during the course of the whole examination. The examiner sees peaks of excitement and notes how the infant's behaviour brings him back to a more responsive state. The kind of intense reactions which some infants demonstrate when they reach their *peak of excitement* makes them unavailable to the outside world, and must be scored high. Others are hardly able to be jogged to respond at all, and their peak is very low. An average and optimal response would fall in the moderate, reachable range, in which the infant could be brought to respond to stimuli in spite of a high degree of upset or excitement, but then return to more moderate states. This is scored to differentiate motor excitement as opposed to alertness (item 10) which scores sensory excitement.

Scoring

1   Low level of arousal to all stimuli. Never above state 2, does not awaken fully.

2   Some arousal to stimulation—can be awakened to state 3.

3   Infant reaches state 4 briefly, but predominantly is in lower states.

4   Infant is predominantly in state 4 or lower and may reach state 5.

5   Infant reaches state 6 after stimulation once or twice, but predominantly is in state 5 or lower.

6   Infant reaches state 6 after stimulation, but returns to lower states spontaneously.

7   Infant reaches state 6 in response to stimuli, but with consoling is easily brought back to lower states.

8   Infant screams (state 6) in response to stimulation, although some quieting can occur with consoling, with difficulty.

9   Infant achieves insulated crying state. Unable to be quieted or soothed.

Rapidity of Buildup

This is a measure of use of states from quiet to agitated state. It measures the timing and the number of stimuli which are used before he changes from his initially quiet state to a more agitated one. Since this implies that we start with an initially quiet baby, it measures the period of 'control' which he can maintain in the face of increasingly aversive stimuli as well as the additive effect of these stimuli in changing his initially quiet state. The first preference is when one can observe the infant as he changes from a sleep state or a quiet awake one (3) to an agitated crying state (6).

Scoring

1   No upset at all.
2   Not until TNR, Moro, prone placement and defensive reactions.
3   Not until TNR, Moro, prone placement or defensive reactions.
4   Not until pulled to sit.
5   Not until undressed.
6   Not until pinprick.
7   Not until uncovering him.
8   At first auditory and light stimuli.
9   Never was quiet enough to score this.

Irritability

(STATES 3, 4 AND 5)

This measures the number of times he gets upset as well as the kind of stimuli which make him cry. Since the presentation of the stimuli is fairly set but some may bring about crying, others even more aversive may not, we have tried to make the scores flexible by counts of number of aversive stimuli.

Aversive Stimuli

uncover	pinprick
undress	TNR
pull to sit	Moro
prone	defensive reaction

Scoring

1   No irritable crying to any of the above.
2   Irritable crying to one of the stimuli.
3   Irritable crying to two of the stimuli.
4   Irritable crying to three of the stimuli.
5   Irritable crying to four of the stimuli.
6   Irritable crying to five of the stimuli.
7   Irritable crying to six of the stimuli.
8   Irritable crying to seven of the stimuli.
9   To all of them.

Activity

This is a summary of the activity seen during the entire observation especially during the alert states. The activity consists of two kinds—(1) spontaneous, and (2) in response to the stimulation of handling and the stimuli used by the observer. A further dimension is reflected in the inaccessibility of the activity in an over active child—viz. the activity is not interfered with by the observer's maneuvers. Amount of activity is graded: *much* = 75% or more of the time, *moderate* refers to 50% of the time, *slight* = 25% of the time. After stimulation which triggers activity, the amount of activity which *persists* can be assessed; *much*, builds up first, perpetuates itself for a period after activity is initiated; *average*, no buildup, and at least 3 cycles of activity which is decreasing all the time; *little*, 2 or 3 cycles of activity which die out quickly. *Continuous activity* is an unusual and excessive amount to be judged on whether the baby can or cannot be consoled.

Scoring

Score spontaneous and elicited activity separately on a four point scale: 0 = none, 1 = slight, 2 = moderate, 3 = much. Then add up the two scores.

1 = a total score of 0
2 = a total score of 1
3 = a total score of 2
4 = a total score of 3
5 = a total score of 4
6 = a total score of 5
7 = a total score of 6
8 = continuous but consolable movement.
9 = continuous, unconsolable movement.

There may be a more marked difference between spontaneous and elicited than this scale reflects. Then, he should be scored midway between them, and the examiner should be alert to the fact that this reflects a kind of discoordination, such as is seen in metabolic imbalance or central nervous system irritation.

Tremulousness

Since in its severe form, this may be a measure of central nervous system irritation or depression, and may occur for metabolic reasons, or since it may be a sign of immaturity, it becomes one more way of indicating all of these. If it is severe, the baby should become suspect and a neurological evaluation is indicated. Milder forms of tremulousness are demonstrated at the end of a startle, and as a baby comes from sleeping to awake states. There is some tremor of the chin and extremities which can be expected in the neonate's first week. As the infant is dehydrated normally in the second and third day, metabolic imbalances cause some tremulousness. In light sleep or as he startles in deep sleep, tremors of the extremities are noted. As he becomes alert and active, the tremulousness should be overcome with smooth, voluntary behavior of the limbs. Aversive stimuli set off a startle which is followed by a return of tremulousness of the chin and extremities. Mildly aversive stimuli should not cause observable tremors in their reactions (see introduction for lists of aversive stimuli). Quivering and tremors are synonymous. Shivering may occur after the infant has been undressed for a period, and should be differentiated from tremulousness.

Scoring

1 No tremors or tremulousness noted.
2 Tremors only during sleep.
3 Tremors only after the Moro or startles.
4 Tremulousness seen 1 or 2 times in states 5 or 6.
5 Tremulousness seen 3 or more times in states 5 or 6.
6 Tremulousness seen 1 or 2 times in state 4.
7 Tremulousness seen 3 or more times in state 4.
8 Tremulousness seen in several states.
9 Tremulousness seen consistently in all states.

Amount of Startle During Exam

(STATES 3 TO 6)

Both spontaneous startles and those which have been elicited in the course of stimulation are included in this. Some infants never startle during an exam, except when a Moro* is elicited. Abnormally sensitive infants overreact to any disturbing stimulus with a startle, and have observable startles for no observable reason—hence they must be considered 'spontaneous' or due to internal stimuli. A startle is scored when there is total body movement. The examiner should discount startles produced by clumsy handling.

*There is discussion as to whether an elicited Moro Response and a startle are the same phenomenon (see Bench *et al.* 1972). For this scoring we assume they are.

37

Scoring

1 No startles noted.

2 Startle as a response to the examiner's attempts to set off a Moro reflex only.

3 Two startles, including Moro.

4 Three startles, including Moro.

5 Four startles, including Moro.

6 Five startles, including Moro.

7 Seven startles, including Moro.

8 Ten startles, including Moro.

9 Eleven or more startles, including Moro.

Lability of Skin Color

(AS INFANT MOVES FROM STATES 1 TO 5)

This measures the *changes* of color and vascularity which take place during the period of exam, *e.g.* the acrocyanosis of peripheral mild cyanosis when the extremity is left uncovered, the change from pink to pale or purple when the baby is undressed —mottling and a web-like appearance may occur in an effort to maintain body heat. A normal newborn is likely to demonstrate mild color changes several times in an exam during which he has been undressed, disturbed, and upset. This should be assessed in particular as the infant comes from a sleep state 1 to 5. The length of time after undressing before he begins to change color is a good way to determine this. Additionally, the frequency-degree of change should be scored. *No change* in color may be the result of depressed or overstressed autonomic and vascular system, as seen in dopey, pale, or cyanotic infants. *Marked* changes which vary from minute to minute would be seen in short gestation babies or babies who were not yet adjusted to extrauterine temperature changes, or in infants whose central and autonomic nervous systems were unable to master the changes during an exam (Fig. 22).

Acrocyanosis should be indicated when there is more than mild, localized cyanosis of the extremities or around the mouth, and especially when the infant is not in enough stress to account for such mild changes.

Paling should be checked when paleness is unusual or excessive.

Reddening might be the result of unusual vascular changes, dehydration, or skin irritation.

Any other skin abnormality should be recorded as it might reflect metabolic or hematologic variations, which could influence the behavioral outcome of the exam.

Scoring

1   Pale, cyanotic, and does not change during exam.

2   Good color which changes only minimally during exam.

3   Healthy skin color; no changes except change to slight blue around mouth or extremities when uncovered or to red when crying; recovery of original color is rapid.

4   Mild cyanosis around mouth or extremities when undressed; slight change in chest or abdomen but rapid recovery.

5   Healthy color, but changes color when uncovered or crying; face, lips or extremities may pale or redden; mottling may appear on face chest or limbs; original color returns quickly.

6   Change in color during exam, but color returns with soothing or covering.

7   Healthy color at outset, changes color to very red or blue when uncovered or crying; recovers slowly if covered or soothed.

8   Good color which rapidly changes with uncovering; recovery is slow but does finally occur when infant is dressed.

9   Marked, rapid changes to very red or blue; good color does not return during rest of exam.

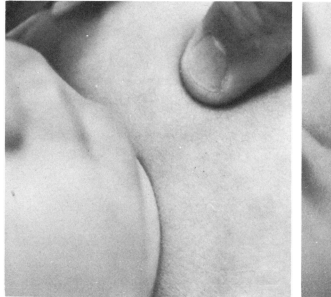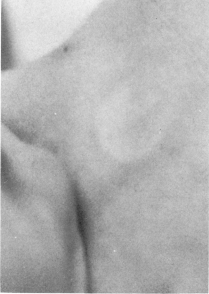

Figs. 22a and 22b. Skin colour change.

39

Lability of States

Some method for recording—a timer, or a second observer—is necessary for this item.

This measures the infant's state performance over the exam period. Frequency of state changes over a recognizable, wide swing are counted. (Sleep to awake, crying to alert, sleep to crying, crying to sleep.) Counting should include changes upward and downward over the exam period of 30 minutes. In the event an exam does not take 30 minutes, prorate it to half an hour by using the formula,

Score = state change multiplied by 30, divided by the length
of exam in minutes.

Scoring

The score corresponds to the frequency of swings:

1	1-2 swings over 30 minutes
2	3-5
3	6-8
4	9-10
5	11-13
6	14-15
7	16-18
8	19-22
9	23 on up.

Self Quieting Activity

(STATES 6 AND 5 TO 4, 3, 2, 1)

This is a measure of activity which the baby initiates in a fussing state in an observable effort to quiet himself. The number of activities which can be observed is counted. Their success is measured by an observable state change which persists for at least 5 seconds. Most United States babies cry or fuss vigorously at some time during the exam (state 6). For those who never do cry, NA can be used. The activities which can be counted are: (1) hand to mouth efforts (2) sucking on fist or tongue (3) using visual or auditory stimulus from the environment to quiet himself (more than a simple response is necessary to determine this).

Scoring
1   Cannot quiet self, makes no attempt, and intervention is always necessary.
2   A brief attempt to quiet self (less than 5 secs.) but with no success.
3   Several attempts to quiet self, but with no success.
4   One brief success in quieting self for period of 5 secs. or more.
5   Several brief successes in quieting self.
6   An attempt to quiet self which results in a sustained successful quieting with the infant returning to state 4 or below.
7   One sustained and several brief successes in quieting self.
8   At least 2 sustained successes in quieting self.
9   Consistently quiets self for sustained periods.

Hand to Mouth Facility

(ALL STATES)

This is measured in all states. A hand to mouth reflex is inborn, and seems to be a response to stroking the cheek or the palm of the infant's hand. It can be triggered off by mucous and gagging in the neonate, by discomfort by placing him in prone. It is seen spontaneously as the neonate attempts to control himself or comfort himself when upset. This is a measure of his ability to bring his hands to his mouth in supine as well as his success in insertion. Some infants bring their hands to their mouths repeatedly, insert a part of the fist or fingers, and suck actively on the inserted part (Fig. 23 a, b & c).

Scoring
1   No attempt to bring hands to mouth.
2   Brief swipes at mouth area, no real contact.
3   Hand brought to mouth and contact, but no insertion, once only.
4   Hand brought next to mouth area twice, no insertion.
5   Hand brought next to mouth area at least 3 times, but no real insertion, abortive attempts to suck on fist.
6   One insertion which is brief, unable to be maintained.
7   Several actual insertions which are brief, not maintained, abortive sucking attempts, more than three times next to mouth.
8   Several brief insertions in rapid succession in an attempt to prolong sucking at this time.
9   Fist and/or fingers actually inserted and sucking on them for 15 seconds or more.

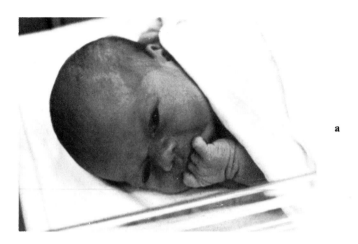

a

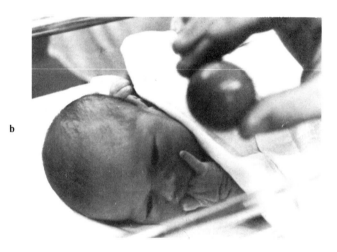

b

c

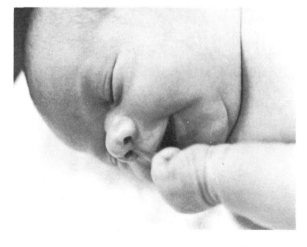

Fig. 23a,b,c. Hand to Mouth Activity.

Smiles

Smiles are seen in the neonate. They surely can be of reflexive grimacing in nature, and they also occur "appropriately"—or in response to soft auditory and/or visual cues. Occasionally, when the baby is handled and restrained in a cuddling position, a smile comes across his face as he relaxes. I have seen close replicas of "social smiles" in the newborn period—when an examiner leans over his crib and talks softly to him. They are difficult to be sure of, may consist primarily of a softening and brightening of the infant's face with a reflex grimace thrown in, and they may certainly be difficult to reproduce. Hence, one hesitates to call these social "smiles," but they surely are the facial precursors of such smiling behavior. A mother reinforces them as such.

Scoring
Record the number of times a smile is observed.
Leave blank if no smile is observed.

Elicited Responses

Many of these are described in Prechtl and Beintema's monograph and need not be described here. Their procedure is followed for eliciting the 16 reflexes listed. Since this is not designed to be a neurological assessment, these will serve as baseline data for a more formal neurological where it is indicated. This manual should score about 80% of babies in no 2, and only 10% of hypoactive in 1, 10% who are hyperactive in 3.

X = omitted.
0 = reflex not able to be elicited despite several attempts.
1 = hypoactive response (10% of babies only).
2 = normal response as determined by Prechtl's manual (80% of babies).
3 = hyperactive response (10% of babies only).
A = asymmetrical response, either in terms of lateralization or segments of body (arms vs. legs, etc.). Since this may be of importance in assessing neurological damage, real, repeated asymmetry should be carefully assessed and noted, to be followed by a formal neurological assessment.

Examples of our use of these reflexes are:
Crawling includes all of the prone responses; head-lifting and head-turning, crawling, as well as hand-to-mouth in prone.
Tonic deviation of head and eye is an 8th nerve response to being rotated in front of the examiner. He is held under both arms; then, the examiner and infant rotate slowly in a circle. Eyes and head go ahead of examiner, then *nystagmus* of the eyes begins to occur, both in response to an 8th nerve compensatory reaction and as the eyes catch the passing light while they rotate.

The 16 responses we study are: plantar grasp, hand grasp, ankle clonus, Babinski, standing, automatic walking, placing, incurvation, crawling, glabella, tonic deviation of the head and eyes, nystagmus, asymmetric tonic neck reflex, Moro, rooting (intensity), sucking (intensity).

Passive Movements of Arms and Legs

(STATES 4 AND 5)

As defined in Andre Thomas, Chesni and D'Argassies, *The Neurological Exam of the Infant* (14), this becomes a measure of consistency and extensibility of muscle tone, in reaction to passive stretching of the limbs as well as the amount and degree of recoil of the limb after extension. As a summary of these in all the limbs and the trunk, it represents the muscle tone of the body plus its reaction to stimulation. A big, floppy baby may have no resistance to stretching of his limbs. A very tense, jittery infant will be very resistant to being moved, and limbs will snap back into flexion after being stretched. Infants normally show some resistance to having their extremities stretched, and a little snapback is normal.

The degree to which limbs must be extended (up to full extension) in order to meet resistance, as well as the amount of snapback (which measures the overreaction of flexor muscles) is scored. Legs are usually more resistant to extension than arms, and very few infants do not attempt to maintain tone of their legs against stretching. Inequality of the two sides is a very important part of this assessment.

Descriptive Paragraph

Descriptive Scores (optional). Evidences for the infant's stage of maturity and dysmaturity should be recorded here. This is also a summary of all the subjective impressions which have been amassed in the period. They include the style with which the infant reacts, the examiner's major impressions about the infant, his feelings about the appearance and behavior of the infant, his predictions about the kind of responses these will call up in his mother, as well as predictions about their ultimate outcome as the child grows. This will be the paragraph which will help the examiner to remember the child later, and may be an important way of categorizing infants, or understanding the scores in the different categories and of understanding meaningful constellations of these categories. This is not expected to be subject to interscorer reliability.

The subjective reaction of the E is subsumed under *"attractive"* in an attempt to score this.

Interfering variables such as light, noise, too many observers, etc. should be scored and listed.

Need for stimulation scores the result of the infant's observable responses. Some infants seem to need stimulation from outside himself in order to function smoothly and well. These infants would score high on this measure. Others seem to pay little attention to outside stimulation, respond automatically. They deserve a low score.

The kind of activity which the infant uses *characteristically to quiet himself* has been of some interest to many observers. This can be checked and/or scored on a 3 point scale.

Comments: Write a descriptive paragraph about the baby which includes the particular characteristics which are of interest in your study. This paragraph serves as a reminder of the unique characteristics of the baby which are not recordable elsewhere. His maturity and any evidence of dysmaturity should be included here.

Descriptive Paragraphs

Five examples of the use of the descriptive paragraph to describe individual differences among neonates are given.

1

This was a well-muscled, well-proportioned, active, responsive boy with an alert, inquisitive face, big dark eyes, and a shock of black hair. He gave the appearance of being 'older' and of 'looking right through you'. As one played with him, he became more alert, and on several occasions seemed to smile as he alerted. He was not fat, but was muscular and square in appearance. There were no signs of dehydration or under-nutrition, and he showed remarkable autonomic stability (skin color changes) even after he was undressed for a long period. He maintained steady states of alertness for long periods. His main feature was the maturity of motor responsiveness that he could command. As one set off a tonic-neck response, he quickly used it to help him bring his hand up to his mouth. After a Moro and the usual cry, he turned his head to one side, brought his hand up to his mouth to quiet himself. Even as he responded to visual and auditory stimulation with rapid alerting and continuous responses, one felt that he had himself under control. A mother would feel that this was a mature, exciting boy, but she might also feel that he could manage pretty well by himself. Striking about him was his maturity, resourcefulness, and his capacity to respond and master stimulation both from within and without. One would predict a rapid, smooth, developmental course for him.

2

This example stresses the individual style of this neonate.

A small, delicate girl with a wispy head of fair hair. She had delicate bones, but was well-proportioned weighing 6 lbs., 6 oz. She presented no signs of immaturity or dysmaturity. She lay quietly in her bed, arms and legs drawn up as if to conserve her energy—when she was disturbed, she gradually began to awaken. As she opened her eyes, she awakened suddenly and became active with movements which were jerky, dominated by reflex activity and jerks. As she built up to crying, she began to make unsuccessful hand to mouth efforts to quiet herself down. As the E talked to her, she quieted to look, brought her hand up next to her mouth and quieted. She continued to use auditory or kinesthetic stimuli to help her organize her hand-to-mouth behavior, and in turn, to maintain a quiet receptive state. When she became upset, her color changed rapidly to bright red, then bluish, but as soon as she quieted herself, her body color changed back to pink, her extremities acrocyanotic. When she was covered, she quieted easily and being undressed was a real stress for her. Uncovered, and unstimulated, she became quickly upset, changing from state 2 to 4 and 6. Unless there was an intervention from the outside, she seemed unable to pull herself out of these upset states. This ability to use caretaking efforts contrasted with her own apparent inability to quiet herself and made her appealing to a caretaker.

Her doll-like body structure, and her immaturity—as reflected by her color changes, and frequent state changes—added to this impression.

3

This thin, wiry boy weighed 6 lbs. 10 oz. He was stringy and long in appearance, had a tense look and tense musculature with little subcutaneous fat. His arms and legs seemed constantly in motion when he was awake. He had been in deep sleep when he was first approached, but he waked up screaming. His changes of state were characteristically rapid, and there was little opportunity to reach him as he moved from sleeping to crying or back again. In order to quiet him, the E had to swaddle him or hold him tightly or provide him with a pacifier and rock him. When a rattle, voice or sudden movement was presented, he startled, and began to cry. He made little effort to quiet himself. This over-reaction to stimuli seemed to interfere with his ability to attend to auditory and visual stimuli for when he was successfully restrained, he could look around and alert to the face or a red ball, or to alert and turn to the voice or a rattle. As soon as the E realized this, his performance changed from that of an overreactive, hyperactive one to that of an alert, responsive baby. But the restraint of interfering motor reactions and the abrupt state changes which went with them was a prerequisite to finding this ability to attend to stimuli.

A kind of autonomic instability when he was undressed and unrestrained went along with this reactivity. As soon as he was uncovered, he turned red then bluish, but when he was covered again, his good color returned. We felt he was a kind of baby who could be very difficult for a mother who was not aware of the need for a calming, restraining environment in which to offer cues from the outside.

4

This three day old female weighing $9\frac{1}{2}$ pounds at birth was a rather fat-looking infant with pretty, round features. Although her subcutaneous fat stores were ample and uniformly distributed, her skin was dry and was beginning to peel. She had lost a full pound in two days. The soles of her feet and hands were particularly dry and scaly, and suggested recent loss of subcutaneous fluids. This seemed consistent with some jitteryness and mild clonus. Although she was not as pudgy or round-faced and immature looking as an infant of a diabetic mother, she had a doll-like look with wide fat cheeks which one sometimes sees. Her legs and arms were pudgy and weak. Her musculature was rather surprisingly flabby and her responses were slow in the motor sphere. She was alert-appearing, but one had to work hard to produce the low grade responses to auditory and visual stimuli which we finally obtained. This dichotomy between her mature appearance (both muscular and sensory) and the difficult-to-produce, delayed, rather flaccid responses are of importance. (N.B. This behaviour might be influenced by maternal medication, but her mother had had but a single injection of mepivicaine as a spinal anesthetic.) When she reacted, her responses were moderately jittery and she startled at the end of a response. This jittery startling behavior certainly interfered with her capacity to respond to our exam. We were struck with her low grade responses, and wondered whether they reflected her best capacity or whether she might not improve over the next few days. A repeat evaluation was scheduled three days later in order to assess her rate of recovery, with the feeling that this curve might better predict to her future development than a single assessment.

5

This example includes an assessment of the infant's mixture of immaturity and dysmaturity:

This infant was seen in the highlands of Guatemala in an area which is very depressed economically, and the mother's nutrition during pregnancy was substandard in calories and protein. This was one of the neonates included in a study of the effects of protein-calorie deprivation during pregnancy. The mother had been 'certain' that her dates of last menstrual period presented a 40 weeks gestation. She had four other live children and three abortive pregnancies prior to this infant. He was a sad-looking baby, weighing 5 pounds, three ounces, 18½ inches long. His skin was dry, peeling, and could easily be picked up off the sparse underlying tissue. The cord was slightly dry, slightly yellowed at birth, and shrank quickly over the next few days. The baby's facies were striking in that he looked like an unhappy, old man with wrinkled eyes and pinched nose. When he was alert, he looked around glassily but it was difficult to catch him to follow a face or an object. When he did respond to a moving object, he followed it somewhat automatically, breaking away with fatigue after a full excursion of 45°. After repeated attempts to awaken him from his initial deep sleep, he began to build up slowly to restricted, low-grade activity of his arms and legs. His state behavior was as low-grade and delayed in its buildup. When he finally built up to a cry his whole face screwed itself up and a slightly high-pitched wail came out. One felt saddened by this wizened, unhappy infant who was so difficult to activate. Even when he became active, it was very brief, and he fell quickly into his sleep state again. His obvious dysmaturity seemed coupled with some dehydration and lack of nutrients. We questioned the mother to find that she was nursing him only when he cried—*viz.* three times a day.

Wondering whether he was also immature as well as dysmature, we measured him, estimated his subscapular skin folds, and felt his flimsy, poorly differentiated earlobes, scrotum and breast tissue. All of these seemed to represent the development of a 34-36 week old infant (as determined by Lubchenko (1970) and Dubowicz *et al.* (1970). Skin creases of palms of hands and feet were somewhat obscured by peeling, but looked more adequate for his 40 week gestational age. Lanugo hair was sparse but evenly distributed over ears and upper shoulders. Nails of hands and feet were long and appeared firm. In fact, the nails were prominent in comparison to the dried, wizened hands and feet.

After our urgent request that the mother wake the baby to feed him more often, and our instructions about sugar water as supplementation, we returned several days later to find that the baby was somewhat more alert and energetic in appearance, but the same low grade responses to sensory and motor stimulation still persisted. Close follow-up of this infant seemed indicated, but was not possible. The infant next appeared at six months and was hospitalized for severe marasmus. Our notes from the initial exam could have predicted this.

Research with the Brazelton Neonatal Scale

Frances Degen Horowitz and T. Berry Brazelton

The Neonatal Scale described in this Manual has existed in several versions over the last decade. Through use and study by a number of investigators, its present form has been evolved. In the process of the development of this final version, data has been gathered to establish the reliability of the scale over the period of the first month as well as its usefulness in discriminating populations and establishing individual differences among neonates. These data have convinced a growing group of investigators that the Scale is a reliable and useful instrument in the quest to understand the endowment, as well as the functioning and early developmental responses of the young infant.

Reliability

Published reports indicate reliabilities of independent testers trained at the same time as ranging from .85 to 1.00 (Brazelton *et al.* 1969; Freedman and Freedman 1969, Tronick *et al.* 1972). In addition, testers can be trained to a .90 criterion of reliability and the level of reliability remains at .90 or higher for a prolonged period (Brazelton and Tryphonopoulou, 1972). At the University of Kansas, an examiner was trained to .90 reliability. She then went to Uruguay for a year where she tested 100 infants and trained others to administer the scale. Upon return to Kansas,* she checked reliability with four other testers who had been administering the Scale in Kansas. After a year's absence, her reliability with each of the four testers ranged from .85 to 1.00. Experience in training testers at Kansas, having them return to their home research base, and then checking reliability several months later has indicated that the reliability of the tester remains stable.

The most extensive test-retest stability data were collected by Self (1971) and reported by Horowitz *et al.* (1971). Using an earlier version of the Scale, sixty infants (thirty males and thirty females) were tested on the third or fourth day of life and then again at one month of age. Reliabilities for each item as well as for each subject were computed. The subjects were Caucasian upper-lower, middle, and upper-middle class infants. All were of normal birth-weight with Apgar scores at five minutes well within the normal range of 8 or higher. Infants with any known medical problems were eliminated from the study. The mean age for females at the time of the first test was 3.13 days with a range of 3 to 5 days; for males the mean age was 3.47 days with a range of 2 to 5 days. For the retest at approximately four weeks of age, the mean age for females was 27.87 days with a range of 24 to 33 days; for males the mean was 27.79 days with a range of 24 to 34 days.

*University of Kansas.

48

For all stability comparisons, test-retest reliability was figured using number of agreements divided by number of agreements plus number of disagreements. The reliabilities were figured at two levels. The first level counted an agreement if two scores were identical or within one point of each other. For example: a score of 7 and a score of 7 were counted as an agreement and a score of 7 and a score of 8 were counted as an agreement. This level is referred to in the following tables as A/A + D by 1. The second level was calculated by including in the agreements count any scores that were within two points of each other. Thus scores of 7 and 9 were counted as an agreement as well as scores of 7 and 8 or 7 and 7. This level is referred to in the following tables as A/A + D by 2. The purpose of looking at reliability at two levels was to determine whether a low reliability at the first level was a function of wide disagreements or whether the disagreements were not greatly dispersed. Thus a reliability of .478 using A/A + D by 1 is increased to .826 using A/A + D by 2. This suggests that the lower reliability obtained by A/A + D by 1 does not reflect totally divergent assessments. Rather, in this example, the assessment of the infant or the item tended to be in the same range of the scale as indicated by the increase when A/A + D by 2 was used.

Table 1 shows the reliability for the Scale scores from three days to four weeks of age for the thirty male infants in the sample and Table 2 shows the results for the thirty females in the sample.

TABLE 1
Test-Retest Reliability for the Brazelton Scale for Male Infants from Three Days to Four Weeks of Age

Subject	A/A+D by 1*	A/A+D by 2*
1	·478	·826
2	·630	·815
3	·481	·593
4	·458	·833
5	·778	·926
6	·760	·920
7	·480	·600
8	·680	·960
9	·600	·760
10	·792	·875
11	·235	·391
12	·615	·846
13	·375	·667
14	·542	·792
15	·792	·917
16	·778	·963
17	·520	·800
18	·500	·731
19	·565	·826
20	·519	·778
21	·462	·615
22	·750	·958
23	·346	·500
24	·630	·815
25	·731	·923
26	·615	·885
27	·625	·917
28	·750	·958
29	·577	·731
30	·500	·750

*A/A+D by 1 indicates that reliability was calculated by totaling the number of agreements (within 1 point of the score of the original test) and dividing this by the number of agreements plus disagreements. A/A+D by 2 means reliability was calculated in the same manner except that scores within 2 points on the rating scale were scored as agreements.

TABLE 2

Test-Retest Reliability for the Brazelton Scale for Female Infants from Three Days to Four Weeks of Age

Subject	A/A + D by 1*	A/A + D by 2*
1	·577	·769
2	·577	·808
3	·454	·682
4	·593	·741
5	·720	·960
6	·720	·800
7	·423	·692
8	·533	·833
9	·615	·846
10	·808	·846
11	·625	·875
12	·846	·962
13	·731	·885
14	·760	·840
15	·640	·840
16	·542	·833
17	·852	1·000
18	·577	·923
19	·720	·880
20	·560	·800
21	·808	·923
22	·680	·880
23	·667	·833
24	·800	·960
25	·760	·880
26	·417	·750
27	·577	·846
28	·680	·840
29	·692	·885
30	·720	·880

*A/A + D by 1 indicates that reliability was calculated by totaling the number of agreements (within 1 point of the score of the original test) and dividing this by the number of agreements plus disagreements. A/A + D by 2 means that reliability was calculated in the same manner except that scores within 2 points on the rating scale were scored as agreements.

The mean retest reliability for males was .585 using the agreement by one criterion and .796 using the agreement by two criterion. For females the mean was .654 using the agreement by one criterion and .850 using the agreement by two criterion.

An analysis of item reliabilities indicated a mean test-retest stability of all items at .592 with a range of .293 to .967 using the agreement by one criterion. At the agreement by two criterion the mean was .783 with a range of .586 to 1.000. In the final version of the scale the items that showed the lowest reliability were revised and some were eliminated. Analysis of test-retest reliabilities on a sample of 40 infants with the final version of the scale is now underway (Aleksandrowicsz 1972).

It would appear then that tester reliability is easy to obtain and that testers remain reliable as long as they continue actively testing. The test-retest reliability over the first month of life is more impressive than might seem from a quick perusal of the figures. The Scale is intended primarily as a neonatal assessment procedure. At one month of age considerable changes have occurred in the baby and it is to be expected that scores on the battery will be different. Despite this, however, a strong suggestion of the relationship between the early and later assessment is apparent from the data reported here.

The Use of the Scale in Infant Research

The Brazelton Neonatal Scale has been used to study both normal and premature infants as well as infants from different national and ethnic groups. Freedman and Freedman (1969) reported on behavioral differences between Chinese-American and European-American newborn infants as measured by an earlier version of the Scale. The sample included 11 male and 13 female Caucasian infants (Americans of middle-European background) and 11 male and 13 female Oriental infants (Americans of Oriental, primarily Cantonese, background). The mean age at time of testing was 33 hours with ranges from 5 to 72 hours. While there was substantial overlap in the range of item scores for Oriental and Caucasian infants the authors reported several significant differences between the newborn infants from the two groups. The Caucasian infants showed greater lability of state while the Oriental infant tended to show more calmness, and passivity in response to some of the aversive stimulation. The Oriental infants also tended to show greater habituation to repeated flashes of light. While there were no significant differences in the amount of crying and both groups of infants responded to being picked up by ceasing crying, Freedman and Freedman reported that the Oriental infants showed much more rapid response to being soothed by dramatically ceasing crying upon being picked up and spoken to. The Oriental infants also tended to show greater self-quieting ability than the Caucasian infants. The authors concluded 'To summarize, the majority of items which differentiated the two groups fell into the category of temperament. The Chinese-American newborns tended to be less changeable, less perturbable, tended to habituate more readily, and tended to calm themselves or be consoled more readily when upset. In other areas (sensory development, central nervous system maturity, motor development, social responsibility) the two groups were essentially equal'. (Freedman and Freedman 1969, p. 1227.)

Brazelton et al. (1969) used an early version of the Scale to study Zinacanteco Indian newborns in southern Mexico each in comparison to several United States infants. All the infants were born without maternal medication or drugs. The Zinacanteco newborns compared to the United States infants showed greater motor maturity, smoother transitions from one state to another and the ability to maintain quiet, alert states for longer periods of time. The authors noted that the better control of state observed in the Indian infants appeared to permit more repeated and prolonged responses to auditory, visual and kinesthetic stimuli during the first week of life compared to the greater amount of deep sleep, intense crying and intense sucking observed in the more labile United States infants. These findings were related to observations of mother-child interaction patterns and to developmental status at one year of age among the Indian children when compared to United States norms.

Tronick et al. (1972) compared ten Zambian and ten American infants at one, five, and ten days of age. All mothers had had normal pregnancies with the African mothers having had no drugs or medication during labor and delivery, while the American mothers had, at most, one injection of a small amount of mild relaxant, but no anesthesia or other medication. Using a version of the Scale very like the final version described in this manual, the authors reported significant differences on six items on Day 1 and eight items on Day 10, with fewer significant differences (two) on the fifth day. The American infants in this sample, in contrast to other samples of American infants, showed greater stability of performance across the three tests than has usually been noted. The authors hypothesized that the lack of maternal medication in the American sample might have been an important factor. With regard to the two groups of infants, the Zambian infants were still scoring lower on items that measure motor reactivity but were scoring higher than American infants on items that measured social attentativeness. Differences in intrauterine nutrition, rate of recovery from birth, and early mother-child interaction patterns were related by the authors to the observed differences between the two groups on the Scale items.

Brazelton and Tryphonopoulou (in preparation) studied three groups of Greek infants and one group of American infants at one, five and ten days of age. The first group of Greek infants consisted of thirty babies scheduled for adoption were born to unwed mothers at Metera, an Athens orphanage. The second group involved thirty Greek infants born to middle-class parents, while the third Greek group consisted of thirty infants whose parents were classified as belonging to a laboring or lower socio-economic group. The American infants included 25 Caucasians born to lower-middle class families in Boston. Significant age group, and group x age interactions were found on different items, generally indicating that by the tenth day the lower socio-economic Greek infants were the most alert and responsive of all the groups. Interesting interactions between days and groups seem to reflect the influence of prenatal history, maternal medication, and early child-rearing practices. These data are still in the process of being analyzed.

The Scale has been and is currently in use with a wide variety of normal and abnormal infant populations. Scarr and Williams (1971) have used the Scale to study low birth weight infants. Sameroff at the University of Rochester in Rochester, New York, is employing the Scale to study high risk and normal infants. Osofksy at Temple University in Philadelphia, Pennsylvania, is using the Scale to evaluate the infants who are products of high risk pregnancies—high risk because of maternal undernutrition and inadequate prenatal care, and Yarrow at the National Institute of Mental Health in Washington, D.C. is studying individual differences among normal neonates and the influence of these differences upon their environments. Aleksandorwicsz at the University of Kansas is studying the early development of a group of newborns whose mothers have had differing amounts of maternal medication during labor and delivery. Forty Kansas newborns are being tested daily in the first five days of life and at Day 7, Day 10 and at one month of age with the final version of the Scale. A similar sample of infants born in Boston, Massachusetts will also be tested by Brazelton and Tronick. Data from 100 Uruguyan infants tested at three days of age are now in the process of being analyzed (Ashton at the University of Kansas). Barnard at the University of Washington in Seattle, Washington is using the Assessment as one of the measures administered by nurse practitioners to predict high risk neonates for closer followup and intervention.

In addition to being used to study different populations of infants, Self (1971) has found that the Scale performance was predictive of later behavior at five and six weeks of age. From the sample of sixty infants used in the test-retest reliability study from three days to one month of age, 21 infants were seen in a laboratory study of visual attention at five and six weeks of age. The infants were shown a checkerboard square four times. Most of the infants showed decrement in looking at the stimulus from the first to the fourth exposure. With the fifth exposure of the checkerboard stimulus, music was played. With the addition of music, most of the infants showed an increase in looking to the stimulus with the exception of one group who showed no recovery of looking behavior and continued to look only briefly at the checkerboard. When the scores for the auditory and visual responsiveness items of the Neonatal Scale were examined, it was found that the infants who showed no increased looking when music was added had had significantly lower scores for auditory responsiveness compared to neonates for whom the music effectively increased their looking times. These results suggest that individual differences in responsiveness to environmental stimulation as measured by the Brazelton Neonatal Scale are related to later individual differences as seen in an experimental laboratory study of attending behavior.

Since the scale has not been designed to give a total over-all score for babies, we have found it useful to think of clusters of behavior which differentiate individual differences between groups and for individuals within a group. In cross cultural studies, a factor analysis has successfully sorted out the groups of behaviors which cluster together within each group (Brazelton and Tryphonopoulou et al.). Scarr and Williams (1971) have found significantly different clusters of items in prematures. Within a culture, we would hope that clusters of items might point to individuality in babies which would predict future outcome. The early work of M. Fries (1944) pointed to the importance of attending to differences in neonatal behavior as they affected their mothers' reactions to them. Thomas, Chess and Birch (1968) demonstrated the marked differences in behavior among individual babies which predicted to their future personalities. Escalona (1968) demonstrates the importance of differences among neonates in setting the modalities in which their environments reacted to them. We would hope that this scale would lend itself to an appraisal or individual behaviors in the neonatal period which might predict to the future outcome of the baby's personality and cognitive development. If so, clusters of items as sorted out by a factor analysis matrix seem to be a most likely predictor (Super, C., Personal Communication, 1972). Single items would not.

Some Conclusions

The above, brief review indicates that the Brazelton Neonatal Scale can be administered reliably by two trained testers and that there is consistency over the first one month in newborns. The data also suggest that the Scale can be used to study infants from divergent populations and may be measuring those behaviors that significantly contribute to individual differences in learning and responsiveness.

The final version of the Scale published here is now in use in more than *fifteen* research settings in the United States and abroad. While it may have been more elegant to delay publication of the scale until more data on reliability and validity with the final version were available, the growing interest in the Scale was a significant factor in the decision to make it available at this point. In the next several years, data from current and subsequent research programs will provide the kind of information that will ultimately decide on the usefullness of this neonatal assessment procedure. If it fulfills its promise, the field of infant research will have been advanced and we shall move nearer to our goal of understanding the factors that conspire to determine developmental outcome. Only then will the visions of insuring optimal developmental experiences for every infant come within our grasp.

A series of training films* will be available from Educational Development Corporation, 10 Mifflin Place, Cambridge, Mass. 02138. In order to insure that data on newborns be comparable across observers and research groups, reliability of $> .85$ across items must be obtained by groups who intend to use the scale as a research instrument with those who are already using the scale. Opportunities for training and reliability can be obtained by contacting those already working with the scale.

*These training films were made possible by a grant from The Grant Foundation, Inc., 130 East 59th St., New York, NY10022.

Summary of Brazelton Scale Scoring Definitions

1. Response Decrement to Light (States 1, 2, 3)

  1   No diminution in high responses over the 10 stimuli.

  2   Delayed startles and rest of responses are still present, i.e. body movement, eye blinks, respiratory changes continue over 10 trials.

  3   Startles no longer present but rest are still present, including body movement in 10 trials.

  4   No startles, body movement delayed, respiratory and blinks same in 10 trials.

  5   Shutdown of body movements, some diminution in blinks and respiratory changes in 9-10 stimuli.

  6   —— in 7-8 stimuli

  7   —— in 5-6 stimuli

  8   —— in 3-4 stimuli

  9   —— in 1-2 stimuli

NA No response hence no decrement.

2. Response Decrement to Rattle (1, 2, 3)

  1   No diminution in high response over the 10 stimuli.

  2   Delayed startles and rest of responses are still present, i.e. body movement, eye blinks, respiratory changes continue over 10 trials.

  3   Startles no longer present but rest are still present, including body movement in 10 trials.

  4   No startles, body movement delayed, respiratory and blinks same in 10 trials.

  5   Shutdown of body movements, some diminution in blinks and respiratory changes in 9-10 stimuli.

  6   —— in 7-8 stimuli

  7   —— in 5-6 stimuli

  8   —— in 3-4 stimuli

  9   —— in 1-2 stimuli

NA No response hence no decrement.

3. Response Decrement to Bell (1, 2, 3)

  1   No diminution in high response over the 10 stimuli.

  2   Delayed startles and rest of responses are still present, i.e. body movement, eye blinks, respiratory changes continue over 10 trials.

  3   Startles no longer present but rest are still present, including body movement in 10 trials.

  4   No startles, body movement delayed, respiratory and blinks same in 10 trials.

  5   Shutdown of body movements, some diminution in blinks and respiratory changes in 9-10 stimuli.

  6   —— in 7-8 stimuli

  7   —— in 5-6 stimuli

  8   —— in 3-4 stimuli

  9   —— in 1-2 stimuli

NA No response hence no decrement.

4. Response Decrement to Pinprick (1, 2, 3)

  1   Response generalized to whole body, and increases over trials.

  2   Both feet withdrew together. No decrement of response.

  3   Variable response to stimulus. Response decrement but return of response.

  4   Response decrement after 5 trials. Localized to stimulated leg. No change to alert state.

  5   Response decrement after 5 trials. Localized to stimulated foot. No change to alert state.

  6   Response limited to stimulated foot after 3-4 trials. No change to alert state.

  7   Response limited to stimulated foot after 1-2 trials. No change to alert state.

  8   Response localized and minimal. Change to alert state (4).

  9   Complete response decrement. Change to alert state (4).

NA No response hence no decrement.

5. Orientation Response-Inanimate Visual (4 only)

1   Does not focus on or follow stimulus.
2   Stills with stimulus and brightens.
3   Stills, focuses on stimulus when presented, brief following.
4   Stills, focuses on stimulus, following for 30° arc, jerky movements.
5   Focuses and follows with eyes horizontally for at least a 30° arc. Smooth movement, loses stimulus but finds it again.
6   Follows for 30° arcs, with eyes and head. Eye movements are smooth.
7   Follows with eyes and head at least 60° horizontally, maybe briefly vertically, continuous movement, loses stimulus occasionally, head turns to follow.
8   Follows with eyes and head 60° horizontally and 30° vertically.
9   Focuses on stimulus and follows with smooth, continuous head movement horizontally, vertically, and in a circle. Follows for 120° arc.

6. Orientation Response-Inanimate Auditory (4, 5s)

1   No reaction.
2   Respiratory change or blink only.
3   General quieting as well as blink and respiratory changes.
4   Stills, brightens, no attempt to locate source.
5   Shifting of eyes to sound, as well as stills and brightens.
6   Alerting and shifting of eyes and head turn to source.
7   Alerting, head turns to stimulus, and search with eyes.
8   Alerting prolonged, head and eyes turn to stimulus repeatedly.
9   Turning and alerting to stimulus presented on both sides on every presentation of stimulus.

7. Orientation-Animate Visual (4 only)

1   Does not focus on or follow stimulus.
2   Stills with stimulus and brightens.
3   Stills, focuses on stimulus when presented, brief following.
4   Stills, focuses on stimulus, follows for 30° arc, jerky movements.
5   Focuses and follows with eyes horizontally for at least a 30° arc. Smooth movement, loses stimulus but finds it again.
6   Follows for two 30° arcs, with eyes and head.
7   Follows with eyes and head at least 60° horizontally, maybe briefly vertically, partly continuous movement, loses stimulus occasionally, head turns to follow.
8   Follows with eyes and head 60° horizontally and 30° vertically.
9   Repeatedly focuses on stimulus and follows with smooth, continuous head movement horizontally, vertically, and in a circle. Follows for 120° arc.

8. Orientation-Animate Auditory (4,5)

1   No reaction.
2   Respiratory change or blink only.
3   General quieting as well as blink and respiratory changes.
4   Stills, brightens, no attempt to locate source.
5   Shifting of eyes to sound, as well as stills and brightens.
6   Alerting and shifting of eyes and head turn to source.
7   Alerting, head turns to stimulus, and search with eyes.
8   Alerting prolonged, head and eyes turn to stimulus repeatedly.
9   Turning and alerting to stimulus presented on both sides on every presentation of stimulus.

9. Orientation Animate-Visual and Auditory (4 only)

1   Does not focus on or follow stimulus.
2   Stills with stimulus and brightens.
3   Stills, focuses on stimulus when presented, brief following.
4   Stills, focuses on stimulus, follows for 30° arc, jerky movements.
5   Focuses and follows with eyes horizontally and/or vertically for at least a 30° arc. Smooth movement, loses stimulus but finds it again.
6   Follows for two 30° arcs, with eyes and head.
7   Follows with eyes and head at least 60° horizontally, maybe briefly vertically, partly continuous movement, loses stimulus occasionally, head turns to follow.
8   Follows with eyes and head 60° horizontally and 30° vertically.
9   Repeatedly focuses on stimulus and follows with smooth, continuous head movement horizontally, vertically, and in a circle. Follows for at least a 120° arc.

10. Alertness (4)

1   Inattentive—rarely or never responsive to direct stimulation.
2   When alert responsivity brief and generally quite delayed—alerting and orientation very brief and general.
3   When alert responsivity brief and somewhat delayed—quality of alertness variable.
4   When alert responsivity somewhat brief but not generally delayed though variable.
5   When alert responsivity of moderate duration and response generally not delayed and less variable.
6   When alert responsivity moderately sustained and not delayed. May use stimulation to come to alert state.
7   When alert episodes are of generally sustained duration, etc.
8   Always has sustained periods of alertness in best periods. Alerting and orientation frequent and reliable. Stimulation brings infant to alert state and quiets infant.
9   Always alert in best periods. Stimulation always elicits alerting, orienting. Infant reliably uses stimulation to quiet self or maintain quiet state.

11. General Tonus (4, 5)

1   Flaccid, limp like a ragdoll, no resistance when limbs are moved, complete head lag in pull to sit.
2   Little response felt as he is moved, but less than about 25% of the time.
3   Flaccid, limp most of the time, but is responsive about 25% of the time with some tone.
4   Some tone half the time, responds to being handled with some tone less than half the time.
5   Tone when handled, lies in fairly flaccid state in between handling.
6   Variable tone in resting, responsive with good tone as he is handled approximately 75% of the time.
7   Is on the hypertonic side approximately 50% of the time.
8   When handled he is responsive with hypertonicity about 75% of the time.
9   Hypertonic at rest (in flexion) and hypertonic all the time (abnormal).

12. Motor Maturity (4, 5)

1   Cogwheel-like jerkiness, overshooting of legs and arms in all directions.
2   Jerky movements and/or mild overshooting.
3   Jerky movements, no overshooting.
4   Only occasional jerky movements, predominating 45° arcs.
5   Smooth movements predominate, arcs are predominately 60° half the time.
6   Smooth movements, arcs predominately 60°.
7   Smooth movements and arcs of 90° less than 50% of the time.
8   Smooth movements and unrestricted arms laterally 90° most of the time.
9   Smoothness, unrestricted (90°) all of the time.

13. Pull-To-Sit (3, 5)

1. Heads flops completely in pull to sit, no attempts to right it in sitting.
2. Futile attempts to right head but some shoulder tone increase is felt.
3. Slight increase in shoulder tone, seating brings head up once but not maintained, no further efforts.
4. Shoulder and arm tone increase, seating brings head up, not maintained but there are further efforts to right it.
5. Head and shoulder tone increase as pulled to sit, brings head up once to midline by self as well, maintains it for 1-2 seconds.
6. Head brought up twice after seated, shoulder tone increase as comes to sit, and maintained for more than 2 seconds.
7. Shoulder tone increase but head not maintained until seated, then can keep it in position 10 seconds.
8. Excellent shoulder tone, head up while brought up but cannot maintain without falling, repeatedly rights it.
9. Head up during lift and maintained for 1 minute after seated, shoulder girdle and whole body tone increases as pulled to sit.

14. Cuddliness (4, 5)

1. Actually resists being held, continuously pushing away, thrashing or stiffening.
2. Resists being held most but not all of the time.
3. Doesn't resist but doesn't participate either, lies passively in arms and against shoulder (like a sack of meal).
4. Eventually molds into arms, but after a lot of nestling and cuddling by examiner.
5. Usually molds and relaxes when first held, i.e. nestles head in crook of neck and of elbow of examiner. Turns toward body when held horizontally, on shoulder he seems to lean forward.
6. Always molds initially with above activity.
7. Always molds initially with nestling, and turning toward body, and leaning forward.
8. In addition to molding and relaxing, he nestles and turns head, leans forward on shoulder, fits feet into cavity of other arm, i.e., all of body participates.
9. All of the above, and baby grasps hold of examiner to cling.

15. Defensive Movements (3, 4, 5)

1. No response.
2. General quieting.
3. Nonspecific activity increase with long latency.
4. Same with short latency.
5. Rooting and lateral head turning
6. Neck stretching.
7. Nondirected swipes of arms.
8. Directed swipes of arms.
9. Successful removal of cloth with swipes.

16. Consolability with Intervention (6 to 5, 4, 3, 2)

1. Not consolable.
2. Pacifier in addition to dressing, holding and rocking.
3. Dressing, holding in arms and rocking.
4. Holding and rocking.
5. Picking up and holding.
6. Hand on belly and restraining both arms.
7. Hand on belly steadily.
8. Examiner's voice and face alone.
9. Examiner's face alone.

17. Peak of Excitement (6)

1   Low level of arousal to all stimuli. Never above state 2, does not awaken fully.
2   Some arousal to stimulation—can be awakened to state 3.
3   Infant reaches state 4 briefly, but predominantly is in lower states.
4   Infant is predominantly in state 4 or lower and may reach state 5.
5   Infant reaches state 6 after stimulation once or twice, but predominantly is in state 5 or lower.
6   Infant reaches state 6 after stimulation, but returns to lower states spontaneously.
7   Infant reaches state 6 in response to stimuli, but with consoling is easily brought back to lower states.
8   Infant screams (state 6) in response to stimulation, although some quieting can occur with consoling, with difficulty.
9   Infant achieves insulated crying state. Unable to be quieted or soothed.

18. Rapidity of Buildup (from 1, 2 to 6)

1   No upset at all.
2   Not until TNR, Moro, prone placement and defensive reactions.
3   Not until TNR, Moro, prone placement or defensive reactions.
4   Not until undressed.
5   Not until pulled to sit.
6   Not until pinprick.
7   Not until uncovering him.
8   At first auditory and light stimuli.
9   Never was quiet enough to score this.

19. Irritability (3, 4, 5)

Aversive Stimuli

uncover	*pinprick*
undress	*TNR*
pull to sit	*Moro*
prone	*defensive reaction*

1   no irritable crying to any of the above
2   irritable crying to one of the stimuli
3   irritable crying to two of the stimuli
4   irritable crying to three of the stimuli
5   irritable crying to four of the stimuli
6   irritable crying to five of the stimuli
7   irritable crying to six of the stimuli
8   irritable crying to seven of the stimuli
9   to all of them

20. Activity (alert states)

Score spontaneous and elicited activity separately on a four point scale: 0 = none, 1 = slight, 2 = moderate, 3 = much. Then add up the two scores.

1 = a total score of 0.
2 = a total score of 1.
3 = a total score of 2.
4 = a total score of 3.
5 = a total score of 4.
6 = a total score of 5.
7 = a total score of 6.
8 = continuous but consolable movement.
9 = continuous, unconsolable movement.

21. Tremulousness (all states)

1   No tremors or tremulousness noted.
2   Tremors only during sleep.
3   Tremors only after the Moro or startles.
4   Tremulousness seen 1 or 2 times in states 5 or 6.
5   Tremulousness seen 3 or more times in states 5 or 6.
6   Tremulousness seen 1 or 2 times in state 4.
7   Tremulousness seen 3 or more times in state 4.
8   Tremulousness seen in several states.
9   Tremulousness seen consistently in all states.

22. Amount of Startle During Exam (3-6)

1   No startles noted.
2   Startle as a response to the examiner's attempts to set off a Moro reflex only.
3   Two startles, including Moro.
4   Three startles, including Moro.
5   Four startles, including Moro.
6   Five startles, including Moro.
7   Seven startles, including Moro.
8   Ten startles, including Moro.
9   Eleven or more startles, including Moro.

23. Lability of Skin Color (as infant moves from 1-5)

1   Pale, cyanotic, and does not change during exam.
2   Good color which changes only minimally during exam.
3   Healthy skin color; no changes except change to slight blue around mouth or extremities when uncovered, or to red when crying; recovery of original color is rapid.
4   Mild cyanosis around mouth or extremities when undressed; slight change in chest or abdomen, but rapid recovery.
5   Healthy color but changes color all over when uncovered or crying; face, lips, extremities may pale or redden, mottling may appear on face, chest, limbs; original color returns quickly.
6   Change in color during exam, but color returns with soothing or covering.
7   Healthy color at outset, changes color to very red or blue when uncovered or crying; recovers slowly if covered or soothed.
8   Good color which rapidly changes with uncovering; recovery is slow but does finally recover when dressed.
9   Marked, rapid changes to very red or blue, no recovery to good color during rest of exam.

24. Lability of States (all states)

The score corresponds to the frequency of swings:

$$1 = \text{1-2 swings over 30 minutes}$$
$$2 = \text{3-5}$$
$$3 = \text{6-8}$$
$$4 = \text{9-10}$$
$$5 = \text{11-13}$$
$$6 = \text{14-15}$$
$$7 = \text{16-18}$$
$$8 = \text{19-22}$$
$$9 = \text{23 on up}$$

25. Self-quieting Activity (6,5 to 4,3, 2, 1)

1 Cannot quiet self, makes no attempt, and intervention is always necessary.
2 A brief attempt to quiet self (less than 5 secs.) but with no success.
3 Several attempts to quiet self, but with no success.
4 One brief success in quieting self for a period of 5 secs. or more.
5 Several brief successes in quieting self.
6 An attempt to quiet self which results in a sustained successful quieting, with the infant returning to state 4 or below.
7 One sustained and several brief successes in quieting self.
8 At least 2 sustained successes in quieting self.
9 Consistently quiets self for sustained periods.

26. Hand to Mouth Facility (all states)

1 No attempt to bring hands to mouth.
2 Brief swipes at mouth area, no real contact.
3 Hand brought to mouth and contact, but no insertion, once only.
4 Hand brought next to mouth area twice, no insertion.
5 Hand brought next to mouth area at least 3 times, but no real insertion, abortive attempts to suck on fist.
6 One insertion which is brief, unable to be maintained.
7 Several actual insertions which are brief, not maintained, abortive sucking attempts, more than three times next to mouth.
8 Several brief insertions in rapid succession in an attempt to prolong sucking at this time.
9 Fist and/or fingers actually inserted and sucking on them for 15 seconds or more.

27. Smiles (all states)

Recorded number observed.

Behavioral and Neurological Assessment Scale

Date   Hour

fant's name .... Sex .... Age .... Born ....
other's Age .... Father's Age .... Father's S.E.S. ....
                        Apparent Race ....
aminer(s)........................... Place of Examination ....
nditions of examination :   Date of examination ....
Birth Weight .... Current Weight .... Length .... Head Circ. ....
Time examined .... Time last fed .... Type of feeding ....
Type of delivery.......................... Apgar ....
Length of labor .... Birth order ....
Type, amount and timing of medication given Mother..................................
....
Anesthesia ? ....
Abnormalities of labour ....

---

itial State : observe 2 minutes

1	2	3	4	5	6
deep	light	drowsy	alert	active	crying

redominant states (mark two)

1	2	3	4	5	6

Elicited Responses

	O*	L	M	H	A†
Plantar grasp		1	2	3	
Hand grasp		1	2	3	
Ankle clonus		1	2	3	
Babinski		1	2	3	
Standing		1	2	3	
Automatic walking		1	2	3	
Placing		1	2	3	
Incurvation		1	2	3	
Crawling		1	2	3	
Glabella		1	2	3	
Tonic deviation of head and eyes		1	2	3	
Nystagmus			1	2	3
Tonic Neck reflex			1	2	3
Moro			1	2	3
Rooting (intensity)			1	2	3
Sucking (intensity)			1	2	3
Passive movement					
Arms R			1	2	3
L			1	2	3
Legs R			1	2	3
L			1	2	3

*O = response not elicited (omitted)
†A = asymmetry

Descriptive Paragraph (optional)

Attractive	0	1	2	3
Interfering variables	0	1	2	3
Need for stimulation	0	1	2	3

What activity does he use to quiet self ?
       hand to mouth
       sucking with nothing in mouth
       locking onto visual or auditory
          stimuli
       postural changes
       state change for no observable
          reason
COMMENTS :

63

Behavior Scoring Sheet

Scale (Note State)   1 2 3 4 5 6 7 8 9

1. Response decrement to light (2,3)

2. Response decrement to rattle (2, 3)

3. Response decrement to bell (2, 3)

4. Response decrement to pinprick (1, 2, 3)

5. Orientation inanimate visual (4 only)

6. Orientation inanimate auditory (4, 5)

7. Orientation animate visual (4 only)

8. Orientation animate auditory (4, 5)

9. Orientation animate visual & auditory (4 only)

10. Alertness (4 only)

11. General tonus (4, 5)

12. Motor Maturity (4, 5)

13. Pull-to-sit (3, 5)

14. Cuddliness (4, 5)

15. Defensive movements (4)

16. Consolability (6 to 5, 4, 3, 2)

17. Peak of excitement (6)

18. Rapidity of buildup (from 1, 2 to 6)

19. Irritability (3, 4, 5)

20. Activity (alert states)

21. Tremulousness (all states)

22. Startle (3, 4, 5, 6)

23. Lability of skin color (from 1 to 6)

24. Lability of states (all states)

25. Self-quieting activity (6, 5 to 4, 3, 2, 1)

26. Hand-mouth facility (all states)

27. Smiles (all states)

REFERENCES

Aleksandrowiscz, M. 'Evaluation of the developmental course of infants whose mothers have had varying amounts of medication during labor and delivery.' (*Research in progress.*)

André-Thomas, Chesni, C. Y., Saint Anne Dargassies, S. (1960) *Neurological Examination of the Infant. Little Club Clinics in Developmental Medicine*, No. 1. London: National Spastics Society, with Heinemann Medical.

Apgar, V. A. (1960) 'A proposal for a new method of evaluation of the newborn infant.' *Current Researches in Anesthesia and Analgesia*, **32**, 260.

Ashton, J. 'Neonatal behavior among two groups of Uruguayan infants.' (*Research in progress.*)

Benjamin, J. D. (1959) 'Prediction and psychopathological theory.' *in* Jessner, L., Pavenstedt, E. (Eds.) *Dynamic Psychopathology in Childhood.* New York: Grune & Stratton.

Bowlby, J. (1969) *Attachment and Loss. Vol. 1. Attachment.* New York: Basic Books.

Brazelton, T. B. (1961) 'Psychophysiologic reactions in the neonate. I. The value of observation of the neonate.' *Journal of Pediatrics*, **58**, 508.

—— Robey, J. S. (1965) 'Observations of neonatal behavior: the effect of perinatal variables in particular that of maternal medication.' *Journal of the American Academy of Child Psychiatry*, **4**, 613.

—— —— Collier, G. A. (1969) 'Infant development in the Zinncanteco Indians of Southern Mexico.' *Pediatrics*, **44**, 274.

—— Koslowski, B., Tronick, E. (1971) 'Neonatal behavior in a group of urbanzing blacks in Zambia.' *Paper presented at the Society for Research in Child Development Annual Meeting, April, 1971, Minneapolis, Minn.*

Brett, E. (1965) 'The estimation of foetal maturity by the neurological examination of the neonate.' *in* Dawkins, M., MacGregor, W. G. (Eds.) *Gestational Age, Size and Maturity. Clinics in Developmental Medicine, No. 19.* London: Spastics Society with Heinemann Medical. p. 105.

Cravioto, J., DeLicardie, E. R., Birch, H. G. (1966) 'Nutrition, growth and neurointegrative development; an experimental and ecologic study.' *Pediatrics*, **38**, 319.

Dubowitz, L. M., Dubowitz, V., Goldberg, C. (1970) 'Clinical assessment of gestational age in the newborn infant.' *Journal of Pediatrics*, **77**, 1.

Escalona, S. K. (1968) *Roots of Individuality.* Chicago: Aldine.

Freedman, D. G., Freedman, N. (1969) 'Behavioral differences between Chinese-American and European-American newborns.' *Nature*, **224**, 1227.

Fries, M. (1944) 'Psychosomatic relationships between mother and infant.' *Psychosomatic Medicine*, **6**, 159.

Geber, M., Dean, R. F. A. (1957) 'The state of development of newborn African children.' *Lancet*, **1**, 1216.

Graham, F. K., Mararazzo, R. G., Caldwell, B. M. (1956) 'Behavioral differences between normal and traumatized newborns.' *Psychological Monographs*, **70**, 427.

Gruenwald, P. (1966) 'Growth of the human fetus. I. Normal growth and its variation.' *American Journal of Obstetrics and Gynecology*, **94**, 1112.

Hoffeld, D. R., McNew, J., Webster, R. L. (1968) 'Effect of tranquilizing drugs during pregnancy on activity of offspring.' *Nature*, **218**, 357.

Horowitz, F. D., Self, P. A., Paden, L. Y., Culp, R., Laub, K., Boyd, E., Mann, M. E. (1971) 'Newborn and four week retest on a normative population using the Brazelton Newborn Assessment Procedure.' *Paper Presented at the Society for Research in Child Development Annual Meeting, April, 1971, Minneapolis.*

Klein, R. E., Habicht, J. P., Yarborough, C. (1971) 'Effect of protein-calorie malnutrition on mental development.' *Advances in Pediatrics.* Incap Publications I-571.

Lubchenco, L. O. (1970) 'Assessment of gestational age and development at birth.' *Pediatric Clinics of North America*, **17**, 125.

—— Hansman, C., Dressler, M., Boyd, E. (1963) 'Intrauterine growth estimated from liveborn birthweight data at 24 to 42 weeks of gestation.' *Pediatrics*, **32**, 793.

Money, J., Ehrhardt, A. A., Masica, D. N. (1968) 'Fetal feminization induced by androgen insensitivity in the testicular feminizing syndrome.' *Johns Hopkins Medical Journal*, **123**, 105.

Paine, R. S. (1960) 'Neurological examination of infants and children.' *Pediatric Clinics of North America*, **7**, 471.

Parkin, J. M. (1971) 'The assessment of gestational age in Ugandan and British newborn babies.' *Developmental Medicine and Child Neurology*, **13**, 784.

Prechtl, H., Beintema, D. (1964) *The Neurological Examination of the Full Term Newborn Infant. Clinics in Developmental Medicine, No. 12.* London: Spastics Society with Heinemann Medical.

Provence, S. T., Lipton, R. C. (1962) *Infants in Institutions.* New York: International Universities Press.

Robinson, R. J. (1966) 'Assessment of gestational age by neurological examination.' *Archives of Disease in Childhood*, **41**, 437.

Saint Anne-Dargassies, S. (1966) 'Neurological maturation of the premature infant of 28 to 41 weeks gestational age.' *in* Falkner, F. (Ed.) *Human Development.* Philadelphia: W. B. Saunders.

65

Scarr, S., Williams, M. (1971) 'The assessment of neonatal and later status in low birth weight infants. *Paper presented at the Society for Research in Child Development Annual Meeting, April, Minneapolis.*

Scrimshaw, N. S., Taylor, C. E., Gordon, J. E. (1959) 'Interactions of nutrition and infection.' *American Journal of Medical Science*, **237,** 367.

Self, P. A. (1971) *The Addition of Auditory Stimulation (Music) and an Interspersed Stimulus Procedure to Control Visual Attending Behavior in Infants.* Dissertation, University of Kansas.

Thomas, S., Chess, S., Birch, H. G. (1968) *Temperament and Behavior Disorders in Children.* New York: New York University Press.

Tronick, E., Koslowski, B., Brazelton, T. B. (1973) 'Neonatal behavior among urban Zambians and Americans.' (To be published).

Viteri, F., Behar, M., Arroyave, G. (1964) 'Clinical aspects of malnutrition.' *in* Munio, H. N., Allison, J. B. (Eds.) *Mammalian Protein Metabolism, Vol.* 2. New York: Academic Press.